To,
Dear Rony and Marie,

In appritiation for your love, friendship and support. Wishing you happiness always. With love and prayers.

Ozzie Sequeira

July 1, 2010

The Alpha and Omega

The Alpha and Omega

Whence From to Whither To

Ozzie Sequeira

Copyright © 2010 by Ozzie Sequeira.

Library of Congress Control Number: 2010906097
ISBN: Hardcover   978-1-4500-9246-3
                 Softcover   978-1-4500-9245-6
                 Ebook   978-1-4500-9247-0

All rights reserved. No part of this book may be reproduced or transmitted in any form or by any means, electronic or mechanical, including photocopying, recording, or by any information storage and retrieval system, without permission in writing from the copyright owner.

This book was printed in the United States of America.

To order additional copies of this book, contact:
Xlibris Corporation
1-888-795-4274
www.Xlibris.com
Orders@Xlibris.com
79155

Contents

Foreword..9
Acknowledgment 13
Introduction..15

Chapter I: Preflood..21
Chapter II A: Postflood History: Noah to Abraham..................47
Chapter II B: Postflood History: Isaac to Jacob.........................56
Chapter II C: Post flood History: Moses...................................64
Chapter II D: Post flood History Moses to Jesus 69
Chapter III: The Present: Who Are We?.................................75
Chapter IV: The Present: The Rise..83
Chapter V: The Present: Fall..88
Chapter VI: Transition—Past to Present: First Proof 98
Chapter VII: Transition—Past to Present: Second Proof........110
Chapter VIII: Present to End Time 115
Chapter IX: What Will Happen after This?
                The New Heaven and the New Earth 151
Chapter X: The Book of Revelation Revealed 156
Chapter XII: Is Jesus God?..165

Author Biography..175

*To my loving wife Lydia,
who has been a friend and companion,
since our marriage in 1978.*

*To my sons Steve and Kevin
for their continued love and support.*

Foreword

A few weeks ago, I met with Ozzie and his wife, Lydia, and amongst other items of discussion, Ozzie told me that he had written a book and would appreciate my opinion of his work.

I agreed of course, even though it was with a touch of apprehension, when Ozzie told me that his book was about religion.

Regardless of religion having at one time played a prominent role in my family's background and regardless of my having always striven to conduct my life with good character and to high ethical standards, the connection to my church has grown loose over the years.

I would also have to characterize myself as the prototypical reader of fiction, albeit that I enjoy a strong historical connection to my reading.

Having now read his work, I wish to add my endorsement to any readers who are as intrigued as I in the historical and prophetic accounts contained in the Bible and the possible connection of those accounts to events that can be influencing our lives today.

What held my attention to a great extent and impressed me is the proof he has presented of the connection between the five major religions of the world, a factual topic that, if received well by these religions and work toward some kind of an understanding, could promote much needed harmony in the world

Now, I must confess that given the advances in the sciences, technology, and space along with the loosening of ties to the church, the credibility of the Bible as a source of information has suffered. Except that when the Royal Ontario Museum opened the doors to its exhibit of the Dead

Sea Scrolls a year or so ago and I found myself looking at ancient records chronicling and confirming the biblical accounts of Daniel and Joseph and much more, a small what-if was beginning to form in my mind.

My life however does not leave much time to do any further research on such topics even if I had the personal conviction it would require of undertaking such research on my own. And as I read on, I began to realize that Ozzie has done all this work for me!

As you read this book, and I do recommend that you do, you will soon realize that this author is not a professional writer. He is also writing in a language that is clearly not his first language. But somehow these things that could have been weaknesses seem to have the effect of enhancing the passion the writer has for his work, rather than adversely affecting his message.

And who among us does not find excitement in the account of ancient cataclysmic events or is not intrigued by the accounts of conflicts in the antiquity of time? And are we not all drawn to accounts of the ancient prophecies and intriguing comparisons of those prophecies when held up against our history, even our current events? Don't we all experiences those what-if questions forming in our thoughts and squirm somewhat uncomfortably at some of those implications?

This book is not evangelistic in nature. The author makes no attempt to portray the message to "repent or die" or make any attempt to sway the reader toward choices the author has made in his own life. The author's purpose, I believe, is simpler. He wishes to share the knowledge he has gained in the pursuit of his own passion and to share his own opinions on his knowledge.

He is not an ecclesiastic, he is not an archaeologist, and he is not an accredited historian. So he is not burdened by an academic standard of proof. He can afford the license to chronicle events and prophecies and to follow the common threads that flow through the major religions of the world and to occasionally, when confronted by the unexplainable, to simply say, "What if?" and to follow a novel train of thought to an interpretation that the professional may not.

I cannot profess that reading this book has had a life-changing effect on me, and I do not believe such outcome was the author's main intention.

I have however learned from this book. And it has gone far to restoring the meanings of the Bible. And it will certainly enhance my personal tendency to always be asking, "What if?" except that I will be doing so with far greater knowledge and receptiveness.

Ivor A. McIlroy
Licensed Paralegal and member of the Law Society of Upper Canada

Acknowledgment

The biblical references in this book are taken from the Good News Bible, New American Bible, King James Bible, and the Bible quotes posted on the Internet. Scriptural references of the other religions are taken from the sacred books of those religions.

The historical, archeological, scientific, and other references are taken from search results in Google and Wikipedia on the Internet and the numerous books I have read whose names I am unable to mention here because of their sheer number.

Introduction

I am not a philosopher or a scholar or a religious leader. Neither am I a scientist nor an archaeologist nor an anthropologist. In one word, I am only a simple man. However, reading is my passion, and through reading, I have managed to gain vast knowledge. This knowledge, I acknowledge, may not qualify for comparison with intellectuals of this planet. But that is okay with me because this book is for the simple-minded people like me. The theme is theologically and historically based and therefore highly complicated in its original form, but I am glad that I have successfully woven this complex literary jargon into a simple, readable, and easily understandable form.

I have tried to use very simple day-to-day language for my theme; hence my younger readers may find many of the words and phrases used herein amusing, funny, or even out of date. Nevertheless, my intention is to convey my message to one and all in the most simple way possible.

The overall theme of this book, the idea presented, the situations and events, the thoughts, arguments, explanations, examples, so on and so forth are not new at all. They are already available in the market, but what I have strived to do is develop them into a new thought theory by incorporating them into one book, thus avoiding the hassle of cross-references into a hoard of books. My reading experience has taught me that this cross-reference task is the biggest hindrance in learning and grasping the truth. This is mainly because, either, the books are not available easily or the information available on the Internet is too cumbersome to gather because the task involved is so tedious that one is tempted to give up halfway through. The result is half knowledge, and half knowledge as we know is dangerous in finding the truth and accepting it or living it.

As the title of the book clearly indicates, this book is about the quest for the truth. Nothing new but definitely not yet understood or explained clearly. The reader will find many dogmatic references from the Bible and other religious scriptures. However, this is not a religious book, and its purpose is not to attempt conversion. The purpose solely is to try to understand the truth of life, its purpose, and its final destination. If I have found the meaning of truth, purpose, and destination to the extent I have, it is because of the knowledge and wisdom I have gained through studying these countless books—both religious and historical and nowhere else. Therefore, I confidently and boldly recommend this to my readers. But to grasp the truth, understand the purpose, and then reach the destination takes a lot of courage on the part of the searcher in the first place, plus a simple mind to go with it and, most importantly, a positive attitude of letting go of one's boxed-in beliefs. The problem with majority of us is that we have our set beliefs, religious or otherwise, that we hold on to no matter what. Many a time, we realize that our way is not the highway, yet we stubbornly stick to it because we do not want to lose face in society, or we do not want people to think that we lack parity of intelligence or smartness or wisdom. We do not want people to think that we are naive in comparison.

Unfortunately, the hard truth is true knowledge and wisdom comes only to simple-hearted and humble people. Whether we accept this or not, this is the fact of life. If we honestly look over our shoulder, this truth will hit us like a thunderbolt. Jesus said in Matthew 23:12, "And whoever humbles himself will be made great." and again in Matthew 18:3, "I assure you that unless you change and become like children, you will never enter the Kingdom of Heaven." In other words, unless we humble ourselves to the level of children's simple and receptive thought process, we will not acquire the knowledge that would guide us to lead a life of happiness and tranquility.

Many of my readers at this point may be tempted to walk away because I have quoted verses from the sacred books. But let me give you a hint—this is where courage and letting go comes in. No matter which religion you belong to or you belong to no religion at all, the fact remains that true wisdom and knowledge can be gained only by reading sacred books. It is there and only there can one gain insight about the truth, purpose, and destination. For the goal of all religions is to lead their faithful to God the creator and toward salvation. But there is a difference, and it is huge!

If we really love ourselves, if we really want to be happy in this life [the need and desire of all], if we really want to make this a better world for all to live, then it is our duty to learn the truth from these sacred books. It is our solemn duty because this is *our* world, and not *I, me, myself* world.

Nowadays, we read a lot about religious crisis, especially in the Christian religion. Either we debate about it with our limited word-of-mouth knowledge (although we think we know it all), or try to argue with our limited theological knowledge, or totally ignore it. The present trend is that we are taught that religion is for the unintelligent, old, and dying whereas science and technology is for the young and the vibrant and intelligent lot. Therefore, the twain cannot run parallel to each other and coexist. But have we ever tried to go to the root of both and try to understand that both can thrive together as long as one does not step on the toe of the other, allow both to live and let live? Have we ever tried to stop and think that technology comes from human intelligence given by God that produces creativeness in humans, and therefore, they can run parallel to each other like the tracks of a train?

> *Ohm! Saha Naavavathu*
> *Sahanowbhunakthu*
> *Saha Veeryam Karavaavahai*
> *Thejaswi Naavadheethamasthu*
> *Maa Vidwishaavahai*
> *Ohm! Saanthi! Saanthi! Saanthi!* (Kathopanishad-Santi Patha)

"Let Brahmam [God] who is symbolized as Ohmkara [Word] sustain and nourish all of us corporately. Let us strive together to amass spiritual wisdom. Let this wisdom that we gather be radiant [shared by all] and holy. Let us not harbor hostility among us. Let obstructions and obstacles vanish from our goal toward spiritual enlightenment. Let peace, solemn; prevail in all walks of our life, divine, material, and spiritual."

Above mentioned is a favorite hymn of the Hindus. It may seem out of place here, but I have included it on purpose because it has tremendous bearing to the theme of my book. I have added many more in appropriate places later.

I believe that the religious crisis we are facing is basically because most of us have grown in the religion we follow. It is sort of forced on to us by our parents who were taught by their parents who themselves had limited knowledge of what they were following. This is because they were taught the half-truth by design by the bureaucratic institutions for selfish reasons. Sadly the trend is still the same. Besides, schools have now begun to confuse the youngsters with their secular ultramodern thought process. Here again, the choice of what to learn is not given to the student but forced on by the curriculum setters. This religious "chaw-chaw" has been causing indigestion and hence the religious crisis.

This caused me to search for the truth independently. The truth that I have now arrived at is that all religions are good because they all march toward a single goal—salvation—albeit by different methods. However, there is one that suits me best because it has unlimited historical proof. I was born in that religion, and in spite of many flaws in its teachings, it still gives me hope for my salvation. Besides, it has many solid proofs, both living and dead, that it is not very easy to ignore the authenticity of this religion. The centuries-old incorrupt bodies of many saints, the apparition of Mary in Lourdes are but two examples.

How I arrived at this final decision is what I intend to present in this book. I hope this simple book will help you, my readers, to find the truth, purpose, and destination as I found it. So read this book at least twice, and until then, discard your old self and put on a new open-minded, receptive self.

Good luck!

Postscript: Part of my profit acquired by the sale of this book will be donated to the Canadian Cancer Society, Canada, and the Seon

Ashram at Ujre near Mangalore in south India where nearly two hundred people—children, women, and men—suffering with all kinds of ailments are being taken care of under very dire circumstances. I have visited this place, and I have seen that every penny that is received is used for taking care of the inhabitants of this ashram. Anyone interested in helping can contact me at oswald_sequeira@hotmail.com for further information. Also I request my readers to promote or recommend the book to their family and friends to promote this cause. Thank you.

Chapter I

Preflood

During the mid-1985 and early 1986, a mind-blowing incident occurred that astounded the world. It was a glorious, happy, and profound incident especially for the Christian world. A so-called myth that bothered, confused, and had caused numerous debates, both positive and negative, was shattered by providing solid proof to the people of the world to see and accept, if they wanted to. God presented scientific proof to show that it was not a myth anymore but a fact of history preserved for future generation. After years of hard work, David Fasold, with the help of highly advanced technological tools available at the time, proved beyond doubt that the boat-shaped structure discovered in 1948 on one of the slopes of the Ararat range of mountains was indeed Noah's ark!

Many interested parties had gone to the site earlier to find out the truth, but they had failed to recognize it because all had different preconceived notion of the whole event. Most believed that Noah's ark was a rectangular-shaped boxlike structure, so they thought a boat-shaped structure projecting out of the side of a mountain could not be Noah's ark. Again, the Bible says that the boat rested on the top of the mountain, so how could this structure, which is almost halfway down the mountain, be Noah's ark, they argued. They probably did not realize the possibility of an earthquake and consequent landslide that could have caused the change in its position. Later it was proved that an earthquake and landslide was the cause indeed. Others had completely missed the key passage of the Bible that says, "On the seventeenth day of the seventh month the boat came to rest on a mountain in the Ararat Range"(Genesis 8:4). So they presumed the structure, which was lying a few miles away from the preconceived and grossly misunderstood single Ararat Mountain, could never be Noah's ark. The fact that a mountain range has many mountains and the boat could be on any one of them may not have occurred to them.

Call it destiny, providence, God's plan, or whatever. It took David Fasold, a deep-sea diver, holder of a master's ticket in the Merchant Marine, a sea captain like Noah himself, to recognize and prove and finally rest the case through scientific method. Surprisingly, he discovered that the boat was not fully made of timber alone as always thought, but its hull was constructed with reeds seven to eight feet tall, stacked and compressed tightly together and sealed on the inside and outside with cementlike material. Only the deck and the superstructure of the three floors were made of timber. According to David Fasold, the construction of the boat is so unique that he calls it an engineering marvel. I believe him because modern scientists and archaeologists are uncovering so many ancient engineering marvels that they are forced to believe that new technology is not being invented, but it is being merely rediscovered.

Why was or is this discovery a mind-blowing reality? Allow me to offer a few explanations here:

Firstly, it proves that the flood story was not a myth as we were made to believe all along. You may be surprised to note that almost all the religions and cultures of the world, major as well as minor, have a flood story of their own although Noah's name is different. For example, the Akkadian counterpart of Noah is Utnapishtim. In Persian tradition Noah is called Varuna; Noah was called Nu in ancient Egypt, and for the Sumerians Noah was Zi-u-Sudra. In Indian (Hindu) religion, the counterpart is called Newhan, and the list goes on. Rigveda, the supreme holy book of the Hindus, not only mentions Noah but also gives a list of his descendents such as Siman (Shem), Haman (Ham), Yakuthan (Japheth). The sons of Japheth are Jumren (Gomer), Majoojan (Magog), Maadi (Madai), Yoonan (Jovan), Thoovalan (Tubal Cain), etc. I have mentioned more names in a later chapter. These names and the later-mentioned names in the Hindu scripture are important for our study because they give solid proof of the links in the four major religions currently existing in the world.

A Brazilian account says that their chief God Monan was very angry with the people and sent fire to destroy the world. But a magician (contemporary of Noah) caused so much rain to fall that it flooded the whole world.

The South Americans too have a flood story, which is similar to the Greeks, that states that a man and his family escaped the destruction of the flood on a boat. Chinese, Japanese, and other cultures have their flood stories too.

The point here is why were we made to believe by intellectuals, both religious and secular, that these stories handed down to generations were just a myth, and not true? As I began gathering information, a question arose in my mind. Why would all cultures concoct a similar false story and carry it through so many generations? Boy, it was such a relief to all concerned when the Turkish authorities finally officiated in 1987 that the boat-shaped structure to be truly Noah's ark. They have since turned the ark into a national monument for tourists to see.

The second reason why the news was mind blowing is because it indicated that there is a just God who caused the flood to destroy the evil from this earth but only after repeated warnings on the one hand yet, on the other hand, in his mercy and love saved one family who loved, obeyed, and served him to create a new world order by literally creating a new world. Besides, God preserved the proof of his justice and kindness for future generations. Could this destruction by the flood be a prelude to the final *Armageddon* mentioned in the book of Revelation in the Bible? There was this first judgment meted out to the rebellious angels that caused destruction of catastrophic proportion. After all, the entire message is the same—disobedience—though the two events—the judgment of the angels and the flood—were different.

The third reason is since we now have proof that the flood account is true, the duration of the flood (not as in number of days and nights) when the water covered the world can be compared to the creation account. Genesis 1:1-26 states that the earth was covered with water and darkness.

Then God created light. He separated the water above and below, and he caused the earth to separate from the water, then he created plants, the fish, and the animals and finally man, in that order. Similarly, in the flood account, we see during the forty days and nights the earth was covered with water, and there was chaos and probably darkness. When the rain stopped, Noah saw the light streaming through the opening on the roof, and then when the water began to recede, the trees appeared. After forty days, the land appeared, separated from the water. Then God commanded Noah to release the animals first (the sea creatures were already in the water). Finally God asked Noah and his family to set foot on the earth. For all practical purposes, the world at that time could be considered as a brand-new world, and Noah and his family as a new creation in the fashion of Adam and Eve.

This thought excited me to no end because it made me accept the fact that this merciful God who intervened to save Noah and his family from the deluge and create literally a new world (and leave the ark as a proof) must have certainly intervened to create a new world order through Adam and Eve after the bigger catastrophic event that took place much earlier. The event I am talking about is the battle that had taken place between the good angels and the bad angels, which had destroyed most of creation. Could this be the big bang the scientists are talking about? There is strong indication both in the sacred books and elsewhere that this could be true.

The fourth reason is confirmed discoveries prove that all the people of the world have come from Noah and his wife and that Noah's sons Ham, Shem, and Japheth, are our brothers and their wives are our sisters-in-law. Genesis 10:32 states, "After the flood all the nations of the earth have descended from the sons of Noah." Unfortunately, there are many who strongly disagree with this by presenting scientific explanation as an argument. However, they forget that science has not reached its zenith, and what we propose to be true today may not be true tomorrow (is this not happening every day?).

At this point, one may naturally be tempted to ask that if all human beings have come from one family, then why are there so many races, cultures, colors, and religions?

The first question can be easily answered. When Noah's family grew larger, they began wandering in groups in search of green pastures, and as the centuries passed by, each group adopted their own tribal name. Hence, different cultures and races evolved. The entire chapter 10 of the book of Genesis bears witness to this fact. Later still, at the tower of Babylon, God mixed up their languages and separated them so that they could spread further into the surrounding land mass. At this juncture, I began wondering, if only Noah and his family survived the deluge and they landed in Turkey and after few centuries later they occupied the surrounding areas, then logically, human beings should have been living only in the landmass consisting Europe, Russia, Asia, and Africa (one land mass). Then how did Christopher Columbus find humans living in America? Or how did the British find people living in Australia when they took their prisoners there? After digging into many books, I realized that humans, being adventurous by nature, quickly found a way to cross the oceans to find out what lay beyond the horizon, and their quest landed them into various parts of the world. Television channels have begun showing scientific series in which they reconstruct models of advanced ancient engineering equipments. Among them, they show that the ancients possessed ships as big as the modern aircraft carriers or as luxurious as the ill-fated *Titanic*. (I have mentioned many more marvels of the ancients later.)

Most of the ancient civilization discovered and recorded dates back to about six thousand years BCE. There is considerable proof that the people of western Africa had regular trading partnership with South America and that they used ships as their mode of trade. It is also believed that their ships were constructed in the fashion of Noah's ark (reeds and cement like material). This is believed to be true because the South American languages have quite a lot of similarity to the western African language. This means western Africans must have discovered America thousands of years before Christopher Columbus!

The idea of building their ships in the fashion of Noah must have been handed down from Noah to his sons and then to his descendents. This means that the primitive people, no matter where they lived, were descendents of Noah (aborigines). I like this theory because it is easy to imagine and believe that Noah's descendents went east, west, south, and north by land or by sea and occupied all the land. Thus God fulfilled his plan mentioned in Genesis 1:27-28, "So God created human beings, making them male and female, blessed them and said have many children, so that, your descendents will live all over the earth and bring it under control." God indeed carried out his plan.

Now what about color and religion? To understand this, we have to go back into history with an open mind. First, let us discuss about the color. If we are all descendents of Noah, then why do we vary in color? Could this be the cause and effect of evolution? I have seen black monkeys, black-and-white (spotted) monkeys, brown monkeys, brown and white (spotted) monkeys, and gray monkeys, but I have yet to see a pure white monkey or a monkey with curly hair! I have a few questions for people who want us to believe that we are the descendents of monkeys. Why has man evolved from monkeys alone and only once? What I mean is why is it that monkeys are not evolving into human beings or any thing else now? Why has this process stopped? Then again, if different living things are a product of evolutionary process, then why have other animals not evolved into something else? For example, why hasn't a four-legged tiger evolved into a two-legged erect, walking tiger? The answer is simple. The tiger was created that way and will remain that way always unless with our modern knowledge, we meddle with the natural process and produce something different.

Some may connect the color to the weather and climatic conditions that some live in. I cannot agree with this because I was born and grew up in a tropical country, and therefore, I should have had dark, if not black, skin. But my complexion is as fair as any European or North American. This clearly proves that my color has come down from my ancestors who were light colored. Similarly, a black person got his color from his ancestors and so on. It all boils down to genes. But the question still remains is that, if we have Noah's genes (no matter what color Noah was), we all should have had one color, so why these different colors? The answer is hidden in the Bible.

When Cain (Adam's son) killed his brother, Abel, God punished Cain to become a homeless wanderer. But to keep him safe from those who may try to kill him, God put a mark on him (Genesis 4:15). Could this mark be the darkening of his skin, which could be easily noticed and differentiated? After all, if one gives careful consideration to this passage, one gets a clear indication that God wanted to punish Cain but did not forsake him, and therefore, to protect him, he may have turned Cain's skin darker (anything is possible to God). Many centuries later, Cain's descendent Lamech also killed a man, and he too seems to have been protected by God by giving him darker skin. This may be true before the flood, but we all know that all human beings, including Cain's descendents (except Noah and his family), died in the flood. Noah was the descendent of Seth, Adam's third son. So if only Seth's descendents survived the deluge through Noah, then how did Cain and Lamech's color survive the flood? How was Esau, one of the sons of Isaac, born hairy and with red skin after the flood (Genesis 25:24)? I believe this is because of the possibilities mentioned below.

Lamech had two wives. One of them was Zillah who had a son by the name of Tubal Cain and a daughter by the name Naamah. After Eve, until Sarah (Abraham's wife), the Bible does not mention any woman's name, not even Noah's wife's name. Why is this? There is strong evidence that the ancients believed that Naamah was indeed Noah's first wife, and this marriage was performed to restore the restrained relationship between Cain and Seth's tribes, which was a common practice in those days. So if Cain's punishment was the darkening of the skin, then we can assume that his descendent Naamah's skin would be dark too.

According to original Hebrew text, Noah had three sons Shem, Ham, and Japheth. "*When* [italics mine] Noah was 500 years old, he begat Shem, Ham, and Japheth." This clearly tells us that Noah had three sons in one year. However, the revisionists have rearranged this Hebrew sentence into, "*After* Noah was 500 years old he had three sons" (Genesis 5:32), making readers believe that the sons were born in subsequent years from one wife. Now this rearrangement (deviation) did not occur because of an oversight but was intentionally inserted to avoid a natural question that would arise in the readers' mind as to how Noah could have three sons in one year, unless they were triplets or Noah had three wives. In fact, the Koran (sacred book of Moslems) says that, indeed Noah had three wives but only Naamah accompanied Noah into the ark. This rearrangement was also inserted to rectify a mathematical error about Shem's age, which caused confusion as to the correct date of the flood. I will try to put it as simply as possible here.

The religious revisionist, scholars, and the intellectuals had overlooked or not given much heed or tried to remember the difference in the number of days of the year during the flood and the number of days of the year during their time. Archeology has indicated that prior to the flood, the year was made up of ten months of thirty days, which is three hundred days in a year. But because of the flood effect, the world began tilting gradually until it settled down to 360 days a year for about 2,000 years. Then again, the world began tilting until it settled to the current 365¼ days. The only way this error could be avoided was by rearranging the above-mentioned sentence. I do not intend to delve into it further as the matter is quite complicated.

This is not the only deviation inscribed in the present Bible from the original texts. There are many more, and there is enough proof that is causing confusion among the churches. Now one may ask, if the Bible is the true word of God, then how can it be said that the present Bible versions have deviations? The simple answer is yes! The original text is the true word of God, but its rearrangement began during the early centuries after they were written, and then Constantinople, for his own benefit, caused it to be rearranged further, and this trend is still continuing. The name of the game is simplifying the text for the understanding of the simple people. The simplification has gone to such an extent that quite a lot of the original text is lost or misinterpreted. If it were not for the discovery of the Qumran Scrolls and Nag Hamadi Dead Sea Scrolls, simple people would never have known the truth about the rearrangements.

The present church is well aware of these facts, yet it is silent because it is no longer the truth-speaking institution that Jesus established, the original church for which the Apostles and early disciples laid down their lives to spread his word. The present church has developed into a multinational commercial institution, which is striving very hard to be politically correct, lest it loses its followers. Take for example the fuss it is making about gay marriage. Let me give you one example where a priest in his homily said, "One good thing that came from the movie *The Da Vinci Code* is that it proved Jesus is not gay." The priest did not mind if Jesus had married Mary Magdalene, but he had a problem if Jesus was gay. There are priests who are gay and who are straight, yet this is what they convey to the congregation. The number of years for a gay man to become a priest is longer than a straight man. This indicates that even within their community, they discriminate the gay priests.

Medical science has established that some humans are born gay while others are born straight—just as some are born male while others are born female. Therefore, the point for argument here is if society and other religions, especially the Catholic Church, accepts gender differences in society, why are they separating and targeting the gay community for their innate biological disposition? Why are they willing to accept other people as created by God and are refusing to accept gay people as God's creation too? Why do they insist on saying that gay people become gay, and it is a lifestyle that they *choose*?

This argument I believe is totally unfounded because unfortunately the *gay trait* in a person is not visible outwardly until the person reaches a certain age. The person himself/herself is totally unaware of this trait until then. By the time the person becomes aware, he/she learns of the terrible consequences he/she has to face at home and in the society and is too scared to come out in the open. I take courage to vouch for this because I had opportunities to observe quite a few children grow up unawarely with this trait until they were in their teens. Those who are bold enough to make the decision to come out do so because they accept the fact that they are born gay, and not because one fine day they suddenly fancy to become gay as many think or are made to believe. It is their inherent natural needs of mind and body (like all humans) that prompts and gives them the courage to come out openly and express themselves boldly. Sadly, the timid ones suffer the most at home and in society.

The Catholic Church that used to totally reject and persecute gay people has slightly changed its perspective now. This may be because it has countless ordained priests who are gay. Therefore, the church supposedly "accepts" gay people but still does not support gay marriage or gay sexual relations. The church presents a time-old explanation against it and "oppose" any gay sexual activity because it is deemed a sin. I find this as a "sitting on the fence" attitude unbecoming of an institution of its standing. What makes one gay is the urge to have sex with the same gender. This is a natural urge and need of all, gay or otherwise. So telling gay people that they *can be* gay but not have sex among their kind, I believe, is ridiculous. I find that by making such a statement, the church has taken a go-between path of appearing to accept without actually accepting. Currently, the church has come out with a seemingly viable solution—training is available for gay people to remain celibate.

Going further, the church categorizes homosexuality as a mortal (grave) sin. It places this sin in the same level as rape and murder. Now, if we look at any of the sins listed in the Bible, all the sins (actions) hurt oneself or another in various degrees. For example evil, greed, vice, jealousy, fighting, deceit, malice, gossip, insolence, pride, boastfulness, murder, rape, theft hurts others while gluttony, jealousy hurts one self. Whereas homosexuality, if consensual, satisfies the need and the urge of the body and mind, and therefore, instead of hurting, it makes the people engaged in the act happy. In fact, it evades many of the sexual ills of the society that would otherwise prevail. Therefore, classifying gay sexual activity as a sin is a drastic irrational concept. With the above argument, it is absolutely evident that it cannot be categorized with all the other sins listed, let alone as the biggest sin of all.

Christians blindly follow the teaching of the church in this regard like in many other cases because of the events of Sodom and Gomorrah. Many innocent people may not know that God burned down the city of Sodom and Gomorrah for their lewd sexual acts (particularly those that involved children). The cities of Sodom and Gomorrah are depicted in the Bible as having no sense of morality. A careful study gives more information that this is because they used to offer up virgin children to the god of fertility. These children were sexually abused as part of their rituals. These rituals were performed both by most of God's people and the pagans. Unfortunately, the city had a lot of gay people, so it was easy for people who mattered to blame them for burning down the cities. Interpreters and revisionists of the Bible in the early times for some reason had either thought it was unimportant to interpret this event in its proper light. This negligence/irresponsible action has been the cause of so much tragedy in the past, and this is still continuing unabated.

I am sure many will agree with me in proposing to all religious institutions, especially the Catholic Church, to stay clear from the gay issue because history tells us that churches' interference with politics has never gone well in the past. Instead, as most of us know, it has created unprecedented havoc. Its current persecution of the gay community is a repetition of their mistakes made in the past. The gay community is not asking for acceptance from religious institutions. It is only asking acceptance from the political and law institutions for their legal rights, and it is high time they get their rights like all other human beings. They are fighting because they are ostracized from the mainstream, so they are concerned about their future, which looks bleak at least for some time to come. I am sure they will be happy if the religious institutions accept them wholeheartedly and allow them to live in peace and harmony.

In conclusion, I would say that unless the religious institutions change their current stubborn stand, they would totally lose the enlightened younger generation of today and of the future. The basic teaching of all religions is love, to love one self and love others in equal measure. I think the spiritual leaders should remember this basic truth and begin practicing it first before teaching and preaching other tenets to its followers.

Want to know what the Bible has to say about gay marriage? Read and understand this clear teaching. King Solomon, King David's son, was the wisest man ever lived. God himself bestowed this wisdom upon him "because you have asked for *wisdom to rule justly* [italics mine] instead of long life for yourself or riches or the death of your enemies, I will do what you have asked. I will give you more wisdom and understanding than any one has ever had before or will ever have again" (1 Kings 3:10-12). This wise man has written the book of Ecclesiastes, which is included in the canonized version of the Bible because the church believes that his book can be safely used to guide the church in its *right* and *true* path. Read what Solomon writes about two men in Ecclesiastes 4:9-12, "Two are better than one, because together they can work more effectively. If one of them falls down, the other can help him up. But, if someone is alone and falls, it's just too bad, because there is no one to help him [advising about partnership]. If it is cold two can sleep together and stay warm [relationship/marriage], but how can you keep warm by yourself? Two men can resist an attack that would defeat one man alone." This passage subtly yet clearly states that gay marriage/companionship/union is necessary and acceptable and therefore has equal rights for companionship and relationship, including all the civil, social, and religious rights. Believe it or not, the gay community will find their natural and rightful place in society sooner than later because God has always been a shelter to the oppressed. This may sound farfetched currently, but if one observes carefully, some governments have boldly brought in new laws to encourage and support the gay community/marriage, and more I am sure will slowly, steadily but surely join in. The United Church, for instance, blesses gay marriages. Here, I believe salutations need to be extended to all those who accept this truth and support this noble cause and kudos to all religions and governments that have boldly brought in new laws to encourage and support the gay community. On the flipside, those who discriminate the gay community, it is high time they realize that they are doing great injustice toward them [fellow humans] and thus disobeying God's clear instructions.

Jesus, as we all know, was the founder of the church and, during his three and a half years of public life, accepted the ostracized community as his followers, as they were. I am sure there must have been gay people too among them, and he being God-Man would have known this. Yet he did not discard or discriminate any one but treated all with empathy and love. Is it not unethical and embarrassing to note that the current anointed church leaders who take an oath during their ordination to follow in the footsteps of Jesus and teach and preach his teaching of "love one self and one another" and the teaching of "live and let live" have totally discarded this prime teaching of Jesus, their first and foremost responsibility? They would also do well to remember that Jesus would never approve of their discrimination with the gay community or any other community for that matter in the name of religion. As I mentioned earlier, the church leaders define homosexuality as a sin, a breaking of the law, but can't the leaders remember that even Jesus allowed his Apostles to break the law of Sabbath by teaching that "the Sabbath was made for the good of man; man was not made for the Sabbath. So the Son of Man is Lord even of the Sabbath" (Mark 2: 27-28).

Sorry for drifting off the track. Continuing with the color trait, we can safely assume that Noah's three sons were born of three different mothers, and if their mothers were from Lamech's family, they would have had darker skin too. Their three sons were married, and their wives accompanied them into the ark. They too could have had darker skin. So we see that the color trait is not the result of evolution but that, which survived from our ancestor Noah's family. Esau's skin color bears witness to this.

What about religion then? The Bible tells us that from the time of Enoch, grandson of Adam and Eve, people began using the Lord's name (Genesis 4:26). This indicates that people worshipped one God even at that time. This continued till the time of Nimrod, son of Cush, grandson of Ham, and great grandson of Noah. Nimrod was the first conqueror who built a world empire, which included Babylon (Iraq) and Assyria (Germany), among other countries. Nimrod is the one who turned people away from single-god worship to idolatry (pagan worship). It can be reasoned out that he is the one who built the Tower of Babylon where God mixed up the languages, which caused the people to drift further into the world, taking their religion with them. So in actual fact, the pagans (as the Jews, the chosen people of God, called them) are also the descendents of Noah who by their own choice followed Nimrod, detached themselves from God, the creator of all, and willfully began worshipping idols. (That is why God allowed the Jews to destroy them when he brought them back into the Promised Land from Egypt under Moses and later Joshua.) Thus taking the example of Nimrod, we can safely say that the leaders of different tribes/groups, which separated themselves from the main initial group and moved away to form their own tribe and culture, formed different religions. They needed their own deities and religion to express their individual identity and their dependency on a personal supreme authority of their own and also to keep their subjects under control.

Now going back, if the boat-shaped structure is Noah's ark, then why are we still forced to believe that the Genesis account and the flood stories of various cultures and civilizations to be a myth? Why did we not and do not still give our ancestors the due credit that they deserve? The answer may be lying in the simple fact that the modern generation (at least most of us) has a wrong notion that the primitive people were unintelligent morons living like animals in the jungle and caves, eating raw meat. Fortunately, many modern discoveries prove how wrong we are. In fact, modern generation with all its so-called intelligence is leading a pathetic life, the rich living in the concrete jungles and the poor living in cardboard boxes and holes in the wall and half the world going hungry. I believe it is high time the present generation is educated and guided to learn the truth. It is also high time that the modern generation give due credit to our ancestors. If we are willing to do this, probe the past with new eyes, an open mind, and reconstruct ancient history truthfully without bias, then what is written in the sacred books will make much sense to its readers.

Here is my contribution in this noble cause. Let me cite a few examples here to show how knowledgeable our ancestors were.

In the year 1908, clay tablets with cuneiform inscriptions written in Sumerian language were discovered. These inscriptions are detailed ancient texts of the Sumerians with which ancient history has been carefully recorded. There are seven texts surviving, and the earliest is the epic of Gilgamesh from Mesopotamia (birth country of Abraham). This epic refers to the Cainite (Cain, Adam's son) civilization, a civilization of Adam's time. Gilgamesh, the hero of the epic, is thought to be Nimrod, son of Cush and grandson of Ham of the Bible. Historians now believe that Gilgamesh and/or Nimrod was an actual living figure, and the city of Gilgamesh is believed to be Uruk (Erach), which is now found under the city of Warka in Iraq, which dates back roughly to 3,000 BCE.

Nimrod/Gilgamesh is also credited with another city—Babylon, an often-mentioned city in the Bible.

The cities mentioned in Genesis 10:10-12 are believed to have been rebuilt on the remains of the preflood cities discovered after the flood. These texts show that the ancients not only spoke words but also had the knowledge and ability to write down their sacred texts and to store them for posterity. It is further believed that there were ten kings before the flood. This belief has come from Berosus who was a scholar in the court of Antiochus I. Berosus wrote the history of the ancient world drawn from the Sumerian clay inscriptions mentioned earlier. Berosus names the first king as Aloros (Adam) and the last king as Xisouthros (Noah) before and after the flood. The names Aloros and Xisouthros are used by Chaldeans as well.

During the times of ancient Assyrians, we read of a king by the name of Ashurbanipal who founded a library at Nineveh and stored the writings (of the age before the flood) mentioned above. In one of the texts, it is mentioned that Noah was to bury the writings in the City of the Sun before the flood and recover them after. In the epic of Gilgamesh, it is mentioned that the hero Utnapishtim did recover some. The epic also claims that the preflood cities including, the City of the Sun, were built by the preflood sages (ten kings) long before the flood and the first cities after the flood, Babal, Erech, Accad, and Calah were built on the foundation of those cities. If Utnapishtim found those texts, it indicates that these preflood kings wrote the old texts. These texts survived because they were buried in the City of the Sun and Utnapishtim looked for them and found them after the flood and preserved them for its sacredness. These could be the same texts preserved in the library at Nineveh by Assurbanipal, which were found in 1908. There is further strong indication that since Adam lived to be 930 years, the creation story and the first 900 years of history was written by Adam himself. Seen from a different angle, we can believe that Noah received accurate records written by his ancestors. He then recorded the incidents before the flood and buried them safely. He recovered them and added the flood story and the incidents of the rest of his life then handed it down to his posterity who wrote their story too, which ultimately landed were they were found in 1908. These records, as I mentioned earlier, were written in cuneiform characters in the Acadian language. There is strong indication that Enoch, a sixth-generation descendent of Adam, was a Chaldean king. Therefore, it means that his ancestors and his descendents were Chaldeans too. Chaldeans spoke Acadian (Abraham's) language. Hence, Acadian is the language found on the clay tablets. Thus, when Moses wrote the first five books (Pentateuch) of the Bible, he surely must have received these records, albeit vastly enlarged by later incidents.

On the other hand, after the Tower of Babylon incident, when people drifted to various parts of the world and formed different tribes, religions, and languages, they too wrote down these texts in their own languages and preserved them for their posterity. That is why I believe all cultures have the flood story, albeit with some differences.

Now let us see how much knowledge our ancestors had in the field of science and mathematics. The most striking example is the first pyramid (other pyramids, I believe, are a poor imitation of the original). Modern science is still struggling to understand fully how this first mammoth structure was built without the modern mechanical construction equipment. For the modern purely scientific and faithless minds, it is still a mystery. But for the open-minded simple people, there is enough acceptable evidence to believe what is written here. According to an Ethiopian sacred document, which corroborates to a certain extent with an Egyptian legend (now believed to be true), Shem (Noah's son) was given the responsibility to bury the bones of Adam at the center of the earth. This is logical to accept because Adam, being the father of the human race, rightly and richly deserves this honor. Noah, I believe, brought Adam's bones in a reliquary into the ark. Later he ordered Shem to fulfill his duties. For the ancient world, the center of the earth would be in Egypt at the spire of the pyramid. So Shem traveled all the way to Egypt and built the pyramid. It is quite easy to accept this story for two reasons. First, the linear measurement used in the construction of the pyramid is the same as the liner measurement used in the construction of the ark! This indicates that the person who knew these measurements constructed both. We are told that God had given these measurements only to Noah, and not to anyone else. Since Shem had helped Noah in constructing the ark, it is logical to assume that Shem too had mastered these measurements and had used them to construct the pyramid.

The second reason is the ancient Egyptians believed that a mysterious man named Imphotep built the first pyramid. They knew that he came from outside into the land of Mizraim (Egypt) during the time of Pharaoh Cheops, built the Great (first) Pyramid with the king's approval and disappeared. Until recently, this Imphotep was believed to be an imaginary figure, but now the Egyptian historians believe that he truly was a living figure. The reason he disappeared was because the Egyptians did not like an outsider coming into their land and constructing a majestic monument only to bury the bones of an outsider. So they plotted to kill Imphotep, and this caused him to escape. To discredit Imphotep, the Egyptians gave the credit of building the pyramid to a shepherd by the name of Philiton who lived in the vicinity of the pyramid. We can therefore deduce that Imphotep was indeed Shem. I believe the Egyptians always knew that the burial chambers built under the Great Pyramid were not built to place the remains of Cheops (as falsely made to believe), but to bury Adam's bones.

Excavations made next to a tributary of the River Tigris have produced a terrazzo floor confirming highly advanced cement-built stones and construction technique. This village dates back to around 6,500 BCE. Now many architects agree that this technique was used in the construction of pyramids that were built later on. They are inclined to believe that the stones mounted on the face of the pyramids were not quarried and then raised and fixed as it was thought until recently but were actually molded on the face of the pyramids by the abovementioned technique.

Another example of the ancients' knowledge is the ziggurat. It is a six-storied structure with a cylindrical mast and a lookout at the top like they have on the ship. It was an ancient Babylonian symbol of Utnapishtim's lifesaver boat similar to Noah's ark. The ziggurat had many functions, but the most important for our discussion is that it was used by the Chaldeans to find the positions of the stars in the sky. It was the northern hemisphere depicted on a flat surface. This technique was later used in making maps of countries. The Chaldeans were credited to be the first astronomers four thousand years before the Christian era. There are few other examples. The Mayan codices are considered to be the greatest intellectual accomplishment of all human history. Their calendar of Venus is the first and the only one ever produced and dates back to more than 3,000 years BCE. The Indian calendar dates back to more than 3,000 years and the Chinese to about 3,000 years BCE.

All the above and many more proofs (more are being added every day) show that the ancients were a brilliant lot. So it can be confidently deduced that they could keep accurate records. My understanding is that what we were made to believe as myth and concocted stories are in fact true historical events (may be made a little colorful by later generations) written by different cultures according to their religious beliefs.

We hear the scientists talking a lot about the big bang. Let us see what the Bible has to say about this.

Writings discovered at Qumran indicate that during the time of Jared, a fifth-generation descendent of Adam, two hundred heavenly beings descended on earth. The name of their leader was Azazal. These beings begat giants on the earth and shared the secrets of heaven. The word used for these giants is Nephilim, derived from the Hebrew word Nephal, which means "cast down by judgment or fugitives." These fugitives (demons) corrupted the humans so much that the "Host from heaven" had to remove them from the earth. In the book of Genesis chapter 6, we read this story. In Hindu Sanskrit texts, it is written that gods begat earthly children who had supernatural learning ability and skills of the gods. Berosus, the scholar at the court of King Antiochus I, calls these fugitives (demons) as Apkallu.

Who are Azazal and these fugitives? In 2 Peter 2:4 in the Bible we read that God did not spare the angels who sinned but cast them into hell where they are chained in darkness waiting for the Day of Judgment. Who are these angels who sinned anyway? Revelation 12:7 and the book of Prophet Isaiah chapter 14:12-15 give us a clue symbolically. Here we have to remember that one-third of the Bible is prophecies, and most of the time, prophecies and visions pertaining to the future are given to the receiver in a symbolic way. "How you are fallen from heaven, oh Lucifer [original name of Satan, Latin translation from Hebrew is Hillel, which means "light bringer"] son of morning, how are you cut to the ground, you who weakened nations, for you have said in your heart, I will ascend to the heaven, I will exalt my throne above the stars of God, I will be like the most high." Thus we can deduce that Nephilim, Apkallu, Azazal, and Lucifer are different names of Satan, and the fugitives are his demons.

All religions collectively agree that God is a spirit being, the manifestation of pure love. Love, as we know, is not static but dynamic, absolutely boring and useless within itself. Love can flourish only in company. With this logic, we can infer that God did not create Satan, the adversary. He cannot because he is pure, and nothing impure can come from him. God's dynamic love caused him to create Lucifer (original name) and the other angels for companionship. Lucifer was a beautiful super angel. God loved him so much that he set him up on a throne to administer the government of God and the angels. God also gave Lucifer and the angels minds that were free to think and reason with which they could distinguish right from wrong and also the freedom of choice. Beauty, power, and perfection caused vanity in the heart of Lucifer. He became envious of God, his creator. So he plotted to knock God off the throne. He desired to become God. Sin of vanity turned Lucifer to use his authority and deceptive charm to manipulate and draw one-third of the angels (millions) to follow him. Thus Lucifer turned into Satan the adversary, and he and his followers rebelled against God. What God once bestows he does not take back, so Satan and his demons retained the power and the intelligence.

The result, a devastating battle ensued between God's angels and Lucifer and his supporters. This battle shattered and splintered God's entire creation, which was peaceful and joyful until then, into a chaotic mess. This I believe is the big bang, which caused the ever-expanding universe that the scientists and astronomers are seeing. This I believe is what the Bible is trying to tell us in the beginning of the creation story in Genesis 1:1-2, "The earth was formless and desolate. The raging ocean that covered everything was engulfed in total darkness." We have to remember here that God had not yet formed the earth; he did it much later. This expansion I believe will carry on till the End Time. What is End Time? We will come to it later. After the battle, God cast Satan and his demons out of his kingdom, and they began to wander aimlessly in this chaos.

What I am writing below is my version.

Surely a little while after the battle, peace must have prevailed once again. God must have definitely felt sad at the loss of millions of his angels. His dynamic love must have overcome his disappointment and sadness, so he decided to make good the loss. But this time, he would be cautious. He would not create pure spirit beings like himself and the angels. Instead he would create man with flesh and bones and compliment the body with his spirit to remain in union with him. Thus they will be in his image yet will not have the power of the angels. He would also give them moral agency, a free mind to think and reason and freedom to do right or wrong. God must have been pleased with this thought and decision because the Bible says that when he created everything else he only said, "It is good," but when he created man, he was very pleased and satisfied with his creation, and he complimented himself by saying "It is very good."

Once God decided to create human race, he had to place them somewhere. Unlike the angels, man would have to breathe, eat, sleep, etc. Looking down into the chaos, he must have noticed that the earth was the right place (located in a favorable place in the universe as the scientists say). So he carefully went through the process of putting the earth with its immediate surroundings (the sun, the planets, etc.) together for human habitation mentioned in Genesis 1:1-25. Here I don't think God took only six days to create the universe. I believe God is not a magician. I don't think he sat on his throne for six days, took his magic wand, and said, "Abracadabra" and brought every thing into existence in six days. I believe God is a romantic spirit being. He would be like a farmer who sows the seed then sits back and enjoys seeing it sprout, grow, and bear fruit. And because he does not live in our time zone, this must have taken a very long time—tens of thousands, if not millions, of years as the scientists say. The natural resources of the earth bear witness to this fact. Thus, when God felt that everything was ready for the well-being of humans, he said, "*And now we* [italics mine] will make human beings [notice the word make, and not create—we were handmade]; they will have power over the fish, the birds, and all animals, domestic and wild, large and small" (Genesis 1:26). Thus, I believe that the six days creation story of the Bible is not meant to say that everything was created literally in six days but just to show that God created it step by step. This thought process of mine may sound ridiculous, and therefore, I would not blame my readers if you think that I am crazy. However, as I said at the beginning, an open mind may be willing to accept this thought process as a remote possibility. The word we in the above passage is the first reference in the Bible to the Triune God, the Father, the Son, and the Holy Spirit, three persons in one God, which the Catholics believe.

The book of Genesis (and many other sacred books) tells us that God walked with man in the ancient days. In our case, he walked with Adam and Eve in the Garden of Eden. I believe this because logically God would want to familiarize himself with Adam and Eve to cultivate friendship with his new creation. Now surely, this must have annoyed Satan and made him furious as well as jealous because if God had left human beings alone by themselves, Satan probably would not have bothered too much. But he could not tolerate God's friendship and love with man because he had lost it and paid the price for it. So he would not want anyone else to have both. Besides, the chaotic universe was his domain, and he would want to retain control over it no matter what. So God creating a universe and placing man on earth and giving him domain over the earth and other things in it (and the universe later) was unacceptable. With the knowledge Satan had received from God at the time he was created, he knew that he would not be able to win Adam and Eve with a direct confrontation, so he used his trump card, his famous trait of deception. He turned himself into a snake (he can take any form because of his power) and played mind game with Eve (not Adam) and deceived her. He knew that if he wins over Eve, winning Adam would be like eating a piece of cake. So cleverly Satan suggested to Eve that if they ate the apple, they would become immortals like the angels who are not like God but almost equal to God, which a selfish God did not want her to know. Satan also suggested that he too is all-powerful and immortal like God, and she and Adam too could become all-powerful and immortal like him. We have to remember here that God had not yet disclosed to Adam and Eve about their immortality. The hint of power and immortality were perfect bait, and Eve took it hands down. Greed must have temporarily blinded her and caused her to lose her wisdom and virtue of faithfulness, which must have prompted her to disobey God's command and caused Adam to do the same. Satan lied to our first parents. That is why he is known as the Father of Lies. This passage clearly indicates that man had/has an inherent strong desire to be immortal (gods) probably because we are created in the image of God. That is why throughout history we read many powerful kings and intelligent people claiming/believing to be gods.

I sincerely do not believe that an honest and merciful God would plant a tree bearing luscious-looking fruits in the middle of the garden and then command Adam and Eve not to eat from that tree. God simply cannot do such a thing because he is not a tempter. God is a lover, holy and true, period. He must have planted an ordinary tree and asked Adam and Eve not to eat from it just to test them. He knew all human traits and wanted to see if they will pass or fail in the test. Passing probably would have given them (and us too) immortality; failing would end up in death. I got this concept from a movie, and it made a lot of sense to me. In that movie, the director intelligently shows one single black current on an almost withered tree in the middle of the garden. Then we see the serpent seductively curled round the tree tempting Eve. The crafty deceiver uses such cunning and captivating words that he easily tempts God's friends to eat the most unattractive fruit. The lesson is Satan and his demons can deceive even God's friends into accepting anything that he says unless man is constantly in God's grace. I also believe that Adam and Eve's sin was not of sex (as some of us are made to believe), but I believe it was the sin of disobedience.

Obviously, Satan was not satisfied to deceive Adam and Eve alone and leave the rest of humanity out of his control. History is full of his devastating activities. He took the form of a serpent to deceive Adam and Eve, but later he began coming in the form of the powerful and rich people to corrupt the world.

Genesis 6:5-7 tells us that when God saw how wicked "every one" on earth was and "how evil their thoughts were all the time," he was sorry that he made them and placed them on earth. He was so filled with regret (not anger) that he said, "I will wipe out these people I have created," so he sent the flood (imagine his disappointment). He had no choice because he could not see man destroying man with evil. He had to intervene once again to start a new world order. However, unlike the two-third faithful angels, he could find only one faithful and righteous family. So he saved them in the ark. Is God to be seen as a punisher or an avenger here? I don't think so. I think we can see him as a merciful God who, in spite of his disappointment, saved mankind. I think we should thank him for not destroying the ungrateful mankind totally and replenish the world with only fish, animals, birds, and trees after the flood. I think that if he had done that, he would have been much happier, considering the present state of world affairs. Will he intervene again? Yes, surely he will. When? When this age ends. When is the end of this age? Believe it or not, it is sooner than we think. Any proof? Plenty so read on.

So is this all a myth? I request my readers to ponder over this chapter carefully with an open mind and come to your own conclusion because understanding the other chapters of this book will depend solely on the conclusion you arrive at from this chapter. A second reading is suggested before going further.

However, before I go into the next chapter, I would like to present to the readers my view about the seven days' creation mentioned in the Bible. I also want my readers to excuse me for leaning heavily on the Bible from now on. This is because the Old Testament and the Torah are similar to each other. The Moslems too believe in the Old Testament, and therefore, the events mentioned therein are easy to compare (if not believe) as a true story.

I truly do not believe that all the living things of this earth evolved or were formed on their own and the big bang initiated everything because even for the big bang to occur, some ingredients must have existed before. Where did these ingredients come from? For a natural question like this, the natural answer is that somebody, a being (by whatever name one wants to call it), must have created these ingredients. It is not too difficult to imagine that this being must be highly intelligent. We can understand and accept its intelligence by looking at the universe. The scientists claim that the universe is expanding, yet this being has kept the planets in their never-changing orbits ever since they were placed there for reasons best known to it alone (benefit of man?). This is just one example. The second is gravity. Even the most intelligent minds have not been able to understand what creates it or where it comes from. However, for an unbiased person, everything around him points out not to an automatic existence but to a creation that was well planned and well executed from its inception.

I do not also believe that, "the intelligence" [God of the Scriptures] created the world in seven days. First of all, God does not exist in a time zone like humans. He exists in the perpetual present (omnipresent). For him, there is no past and no future, only the present. That is why time (as we figure it on Earth) does not exist in the outer space. Thus, our seven days could have been God's seven million years. Besides, like I said earlier, I do not believe that God sat on his throne for six days in a row, took his wand, and magically created the world, and then he was so tired that he took a rest on the seventh day. Not that he couldn't do these things but because he wouldn't enjoy his magic creation. He took a lot of trouble to carefully design each of his creation, and that is why he loves everyone and everything so dearly. The Bible tells us that after each of his creation, he said "good" and "very good," which means that he was delighted in his creation. What I believe is that he must have taken his own sweet time to put things together. The seven days mentioned in the Bible is just to show that God created things step by step and in a certain order.

Genesis 2:3 tells us that God stopped working (rested) on the seventh day, blessed it, and set it apart as a special day. This makes one to think (and is understood that way) that God needed rest, so he set apart one day for himself. The truth of the matter, I believe, is that God did not set apart a day for himself but for the people in our timeframe, which later would be called the day of Sabbath. I think it is appropriate to mention here that God did not mention the days by name at all when he established them. We come across the word Sabbath much later in Exodus 20:8-11 when at

Mount Sinai God gives the Ten Commandments to Moses. Consequently, all the controversy about Sabbath being the seventh day of the week, from sundown on Friday to sundown on Saturday for the Jews and Sunday for the Christians, seems baseless. Especially, as mentioned above, if we believe God took his own time, then there is no meaning for the much-debated seven days. What I believe is that God expects us to keep one day for his worship according to our convenience. However, because humans are social animals who like to group together to perform all chores, this worship seemed appropriate to be held in community initially, which became an accepted rule later. For this, a common day was appointed that was suitable, appropriate, and beneficial to all. Since Sunday was and is accepted as a common holiday in most parts of the world, the worship began to be held on that day. This, I believe, has nothing to do with the church following/borrowing the ancient pagan "Sun day" as many argue. Unfortunately, people's ignorance makes them believe that God responds to our prayers only if we worship him on a Sabbath (for Jews) a Sunday (for Christians) or a Friday (for Moslems). I truly believe that he will really care and will be displeased if we do not worship him once a week at least and take rest on that day. I believe my argument holds firm ground if we consider the fact that in the Moslem countries, the weekly holiday is Friday, so those Christians who cannot observe their Sunday obligation are allowed to do so on Friday. Will God punish these millions? The church has given special permission for this. How could the church, which is supposed to be striving to follow God's commandments strictly, make this adjustment? Is it not because the church believes that God is not a taskmaster who sticks to his rule no matter what? Is it not because the church believes that "Sabbath is made for man and not man is made for Sabbath"?

It is also very saddening to note the tussle going on in the church about the Sunday, Christmas Day, Easter day, etc, not being recognized (celebrated) by the early church. Some denominations claim that the Catholic and some other churches have borrowed these festivals and the days from the pagans, and therefore, they are an abomination to the sacred services of the church. I have lived in many parts of the world, and I have not seen any other religion currently celebrating any of their festivals on any of those days. Thus, even if Christianity has borrowed these days from the pagan world, would God really care? Did he not create the days himself, and therefore, do they not all belong to him?

Another thought. I would like to believe that God did not create everything in only six days because, as I said earlier, he is not a magician. He is a romantic being. I would like to believe that he would like to see his creation grow, flourish, and bear fruit in front of his eyes like for example a farmer who would sow the seed and wait and watch for it to grow and bear fruit with great joy. God loved the human race so much that he wanted to give us everything, all the resources of this world and the outer world for our happiness. He wanted to keep everything ready for us before he brought us into existence by natural process so that he could enjoy watching us using his gifts intelligently. He must have taken tens of thousands of years (by human standards) to put everything in order. Finally, when he was satisfied, he created Adam alone to see how he would interact with his surroundings. When God found that none was suitable for Adam's companionship, he created Eve. So the conflict between religious beliefs and the scientific thought process, which is wide and growing wider every day, should be stopped once for all. Instead, they should be allowed to coexist in an amicable way for the benefit of all.

Chapter II A

Postflood History: Noah to Abraham

One of the purposes of this book is to try and understand the beginning and the final destination of man, alpha and omega. In pursuing this goal, it is obviously necessary to start from the beginning—the starting point. Whether we believe that God created human beings or we follow Darwin's theory of evolution, the fact remains that there has to be a starting point when a fully developed man with human faculties appeared on this earth. While Darwin could not give an approximate time, the Bible and other religious sources give the approximate time as little less than 6000 years. There is however disagreement about this. The book of Genesis 5:1-31, from Adam to Noah, gives us a count of 1,556 years while other Christian sources give us a count of 2,262 years. This disagreement could be because of miscalculations made in the earlier ages about the number of days in a calendar year of ancient period. Archaeologists are now agreeing that before the deluge, the year had 300 days. Then during the deluge, the Earth tilted a few degrees, and the number of days of the year advanced to 360 days. This remained for about 2,000 years and, then again the earth tilted a little, and now we have 365¼ days. This count of 6,000 years of world order and 1,000 years of Jesus' reign equaling to 7,000 years of the Bible seems to be acceptable because Barosus, the scholar, came out with a calculation of 1,440 years from Adam to Noah, which is close to the Genesis account. So if we take the count from Adam to Noah as 1,556, then from

Noah to Jesus, the Bible gives an account of 2,303 years (details given in a later chapter). We are in 2010. If we add 1,556+2,303+2,010, we get a figure of 5,869, which is close to 6,000years. This 6,000 years is significant because at the end of the 6,000th year, the battle of Armageddon will take place, when two-thirds of the earth will be destroyed; then Jesus will come again and rule the world for a thousand years. 6,000+1,000=7,000 years. More about this is explained in a later chapter.

I found that it was not necessary for me to know when Adam was born or when the flood occurred, but it was necessary for me to know and accept that the superheroes of the Old Testament did indeed walk on this earth and to know the way they were instrumental in shaping the course of life from the beginning up to this day. It was also necessary to know that the flood did occur at a certain point in time in history and thus to know my beginning and my final destiny and the destiny of all human beings.

Since we have gathered enough historical proof from Adam to Noah, we now have to proceed from Noah to Abram, son of Terah. This is because up to the time of Abram; God sort of directly controlled human activity. But after God made his first covenant with Abram (he made five covenants in all with Abram, Genesis 12:1-3, 15:1-5, 17:1-22, 18:9-10, and 22:15-18) God kind of took a backseat and made man to do his own work though he intervened and guided man whenever necessary. We can understand this easily from the Bible because for about four hundred years after the flood until the time of Nimrod, people worshipped one God. But Nimrod, with his power and might, drew the people into pagan worship. Noticing that evil was once again spreading on earth and people were once again heading for disaster, God mixed up the peoples' languages at the Tower of Babylon and caused them to spread out. Then according to his plan, he decided to use man to handle their destiny on their own, which is continuing till today. His original plan was that he would be our God, and we would be his people, but disobedience once again caused him to change his mind. However he would not disown us but take a backseat and guide us lead us and intervene in our affairs only when absolutely necessary.

For this purpose, God chose Abram to establish a nation dear to his heart. That is why God inspired St. Peter in his first letter, 1 Peter 2:9, to call it "a holy nation, a royal priesthood, a people set apart." That is why God called this nation "out of darkness into his marvelous light." Peter had written this letter to the suffering Christians scattered throughout the northern part of Asia Minor. These people are called God's chosen people in his letter. (Also read Exodus 19:5-6, Isaiah 9:2, 43:20-21, Deuteronomy 4:20:7, 6:14:2, Titus 2:14.)

It may be surprising to note that God chose Abram, a pagan, to establish his nation. Surely, there must have been righteous people among his own worshippers. I believe this was because God wanted to establish the truth right from the beginning that he can and will use any one he wishes to do his work no matter what religion, cast, color, and race that person may belong to. Also we have to understand that to do his work, he chooses people in their mother's womb, and no matter what lifestyle they live, when the time comes, he calls them for his service. The Bible has many examples, Noah, Jacob and his son Joseph, Moses, and the prophets before Jesus. After Jesus, there were Apostles and the disciples—the most prominent among them was St. Paul—and then there were the beatified saints, Mother Teresa being the most recent one. For God, all are his children, and he does not discriminate. He chose the nation of Israel specifically because he wanted to mould it into a model nation so that others would see the difference and follow. That is why he gave them the commandments and statutes. Unfortunately, that nation has failed so far. Also Jesus was to be born from this nation.

I believe that there is another reason why God chose Abram. Abram was the descendent of Shem (Noah's son). Like Noah, Shem was saved from the flood and brought into the new world because of his righteousness. Down the line some of Shem's descendents followed Nimrod and adapted paganism, so by the time Nahor, Noah's grandson, was born, paganism had become their natural (birth) religion. Thus, Tehra, Abram's father, and Abram were pagans—not by choice.

This makes one realize one vital and gracious fact about God. That is, God knows and understands that from ancient times up until now, people have been following a certain religion not necessarily by their own choice but either by a natural way through the ancestors or voluntary or forced conversion. We all know that forced conversion has been part of our history. God definitely does not like this, and he also definitely loathes people who proclaim themselves to be gods and start their own religion for selfish reasons and thus create havoc in the name of religion.

Therefore, since God understands the plight of ordinary people, all he expects us to do is to lead a good life according to his statutes to the best of our ability. Fortunately, all religions have their God-given statutes inscribed in their sacred books.

For these humanly understandable and many not so clearly understandable reasons to humans, God chose Abram as his instrument. Until recently, we were made to believe that Abram and his ancestors were uneducated nomads wandering from place to place. But now, there is strong evidence that their household was firmly established in Ur of Babylonia, and they were wealthy people manufacturing and trading in statues, a lucrative business at the time, as the community was idol worshippers. It is also established that Abram was a well-educated person helping out in his father's business.

If we see the map of the ancient world in the Bible, we find that Ur is situated at the southwest tip of Babylonia in the southern part of Mesopotamia while Haran is way up in the north and Canaan is way out to the west on the coast of the Mediterranean Sea.

Genesis 11:31-32 says, Terah took his son Abram, his grandson Lot, who was the son of Haran (the city of Haran was named after him), and his daughter-in-law Sarai, Abram's wife (who was named Sarah later) and, with them, left the city of Ur in Babylonia to go to the land of Canaan. They went as far as Haran and settled there. Terah died there at the age of 205.

Again Genesis 12:4-5 says, when Abram was seventy-five years old, he started from Haran as the Lord had told him to do, and Lot went with him. Abram took his wife Sarai and nephew Lot and all the wealth and the slaves they had acquired in Haran, and they started out for the land of Canaan.

One may be inclined to wonder here as to why did Abram go or why did God allow Abram to go all the way north to Haran from Ur when Abram could have crossed the desert and gone west straight to Canaan? I would like to believe that there were two specific reasons.

First, as we know Terah, Abram's father, had three sons, Abram, Nahor, and Haran. Abram, being the firstborn, had remained with Terah while Nahor and Haran had moved out to establish their own household. Haran settled down in north Mesopotamia and named the city as Haran after himself. However, Haran died, and his son Lot began living with Abram and his grandfather Terah at Ur. Although no mention is made directly in the Bible regarding the place where Nahor had settled down, Genesis 24:10 gives us a clue that he too had settled down in northern Mesopotamia because seventy years later, Abram sent his servant to northern Mesopotamia to look for a wife for Isaac from among his own people. The servant landed in the house of Bethuel, son of Nahor, father of Rebecca. Rebecca became Isaac's wife later.

So when God instructed Abram to go to Canaan, a faraway and an unknown land, to establish a new nation, both Terah and Abram would naturally want all their kith and kin to accompany them to the Promised Land (family ties being very strong in those days). So they went to Haran. The Bible indicates that they lived there for quite a long time because Genesis 12:5 says that Abram took his wife Sarai, his nephew Lot, and all the wealth, and all the slaves they had acquired in Haran and started out for the land of Canaan. So now we know the first reason.

The second reason I would like to believe why God allowed Abram to go to Haran is God was marking (defining) the territory that he would give as an inheritance to Abram and his descendents. If we carefully follow Abram's life journey, we can get a gist of this. What gives me the courage to write this is the passage in Genesis 13:14, which says, after Lot left, the Lord said to Abram, "From where you are, look carefully in all directions. I am going to give you and your descendents all the land that you see and it will be yours forever. I will give you so many descendents that no one will be able to count them all. It would be easy to count all the specks of dust on the earth! Now go and look over the whole land, because I am going to give it to you."

Dear reader, I urge you to remember this promise to Abram and the five covenants mentioned after two paragraphs during your entire reading because God's plan and man's destiny will be revealed piecemeal through this book by virtue of these promises!

Thus, this passage clearly reveals that God gave the Promised Land to his chosen people during the time of Abram, and although others would occupy it during their absence while they were in captivity for 430 years in Egypt, God would bring them back through Moses and Aaron and settle them back in their land once again (read Deuteronomy 32:48-52 and 34:1-4). Therefore, the land belonged to Abram, before and after God changed his name, and his descendents. All other claims, I believe, are spurious, born out of lack of biblical/historical knowledge and greed. Study the map of the ancient world in the Bible for confirmation.

Earlier in this chapter, I had mentioned that God made five covenants with Abram. We have to understand here that they were not five different covenants but sort of improvisations from the previous to the next. Let us take a look at the five covenants:

First Covenant: Genesis 12:1-3. The Lord said to Abram, "Leave your country, and your father's home and go to the land that I am going to show you. I will give you many descendents and they will become a great nation. I will bless you and make your name famous, so that you will be a blessing. I will bless those who bless you, but I will curse those who curse you and through you I will bless all the nations." This is very encouraging yet must have sounded hopelessly stupid to Abram, a man of advanced age without his own children!

Second Covenant: Genesis 15:1-21. After this, Abram had a vision and heard the Lord say to him, "Do not be afraid, Abram, I will shield you from danger and give you great reward." Abram's reply shows irritation when he says, "Sovereign Lord, what good will your reward do to me, since I have no children? My only heir is Eliezer of Damascus. You have given me no children and one of my slaves will inherit my property." In other words, Abram was saying, "Are you kidding me? How are you going to make a great nation out of me without my own child? How can I be sure that the land you are going to give me will be mine and my descendents forever?" The rest of the chapter shows how God assures Abram not only with a promise of an heir but he also reaffirms his previous covenant by asking Abram to sacrifice a cow, goat, and a ram. This act of God must have satisfied Abram, so as per Genesis 15:6, Abram put his trust in the

Lord, and because of this, the Lord was pleased with him and accepted him. The words accepted him, I believe, are very important because I think it was then that God actually trusted in Abram's faithfulness and decided to bring him out of paganism into his own marvelous light and make him the builder of his holy nation. The next covenant clearly shows this. However, God wanted Abram to know that all will not be hunky-dory with his descendents. God wanted to show Abram that he was the God of the past, the present, and the future. Therefore, God puts Abram into a deep sleep and shows him what will happen to his descendents in the future in a dream. But then, God also gives Abram hope and assurance of a good future under certain conditions.

Third Covenant: Genesis: 17:1-27 tells us that when Abram was ninety-nine years old, God appeared to Abram again. However, twenty-four years had passed since the previous covenant, and nothing concrete had taken place. Sarai gets disappointed and fed up waiting all those years and asks Abram to sleep with Hagar, her maid, who gives birth to Ishmael through this relationship. Abram must have agreed to this because he too must have thought that God has forgotten his covenant. He was not in a position to wait any longer as age was catching up. But God's ways are not our ways! He has his own plans, which may look unrealistic to humans. So when he appears to Abram this time, he not only renews his promise but also anoints Abram with a new name. He renames him as Abraham, which means "ancestor of many nations," instead of his previous name Abram. Further, God elaborates his covenant with the promise of a son and even names him Isaac. God also changes Sarai's name to Sarah, which means "mother of nations." Though Abraham doubts and asks God to make Ishmael as his heir, God does not get angry, instead shows his justice by promising to bless Ishmael with twelve princes and make a great nation out of him (the current Ishmaelite clan are the descendents of Ishmael). Here we have to remember that though Ishmael was the firstborn of Abraham, he was born to a slave, and a slave's child though firstborn could not be the receiver of an inheritance. Yet God blesses Ishmael because he was Abraham's blood and God's justice is great! Another aspect we have to know here is that though Hagar is mentioned as a slave in the Bible, she was not a slave in the real sense but a princess, a daughter of a pharaoh. Sarah had befriended Hagar when she was living in Egypt. They had grown so close to each other that Hagar had accompanied Sarah when she came back to Canaan.

Going back to the covenant, we see that God needed a guarantee from Abraham too because humans are humans after all—they have a free will and are capable of changing their minds any time. So God told Abraham that he would seal this covenant through the act of circumcision. But he warned Abraham that his promise would remain effective only as long as Abraham and his descendents kept their part of the bargain. The guarantee that God asked of Abraham was circumcision of all the male members of the household forever. Though we find Abraham laughing secretly at God earlier, somehow he seemed to have believed on this occasion because he got Ishmael and himself and all the other males in the household circumcised on one single day. God must have been extremely happy that day because his plan of building a holy nation was taking shape at last.

Fourth covenant: According to Genesis 18, the Lord "appeared" to Abraham once again at the sacred trees of Mamre on the way to Sodom and Gomorrah and renewed his promise that Sarah will bear a child. Though Sarah laughs and Abraham voices his doubt, God promises that in nine months' time, Sarah will give birth to a male child. This time, there is no delay; Sarah becomes pregnant and gives birth to Isaac. The word appeared at the beginning of the paragraph should be taken not as in appeared in a dream but as in appeared personally because Genesis 18:2 says that Abraham looked up and saw three men standing there. Then Genesis 18:22 says that two men left and went to Sodom and Gomorrah. I would like to understand this in two ways. God intentionally came down to meet Abraham and bless Sarah personally, but he brought two angels to deal with the problem of Sodom and Gomorrah. The second is God was showing that he does not appear only in dreams and visions or talk from the clouds, but he can and would come down to earth in human form to be with humans whenever necessary, like Jesus Christ many centuries later.

Fifth covenant: In Genesis 22, God talks to Abraham on two occasions, first, to ask him to offer his son Isaac as a sacrifice. This was a severe test of course, a test not so much for God for his personal satisfaction but for Abraham for his obedience and faith. Abraham passes this test with flying colors, and the history of the world was changed forever. We have to thank and appreciate Abraham for his faith and obedience because let's just wear Abraham's shoes and stand in his position for a moment. Sarah and Hagar had a problem and Abraham had to send Hagar and Ishmael away (I am sure Abraham loved them dearly too) never to return, which means that Abraham would lose his firstborn forever. In this sad situation, a seemingly cruel God asks Abraham to sacrifice his only remaining son through whom God had promised him the moon and the stars. Somehow Abraham seems to have developed tremendous faith in God probably because God had kept his promise and done the impossible by giving him a son at such an advanced age. So Abraham gathers enough courage and goes to do God's bidding. Here, God seems to be teaching us a lesson, that is, even in the worst situation, God gives us courage if we have faith as big as a mustard seed and shows us a way out, sometimes in miraculous ways. This truth is established when God provides a lamb out of nowhere for sacrifice in place of Isaac.

These five covenants, though made at different times, should be considered as one and the same, made at different stages with specific reasons and on them is built the human history of the past, all the current happenings, and believe it or not, the consequences of the future will depend on them as well.

One-third of the Bible contains prophecies. Though some of them were given for the particular time, most of them were given for the future with dual purpose. If we follow the world events carefully, we will be surprised to note that many of the events mentioned in them have taken place accurately and on time. Unfortunately, most of these prophecies are symbolically written and difficult to understand.

In the rest of the book, we will try to decipher these symbols and thus understand its significance and correctness. We will also discuss in detail the five covenants, their relevance to the current situation, and their connection with the future.

Chapter II B

Postflood History: Isaac to Jacob

From Abraham, we move on to Isaac. Nothing exciting happens in his personal life except that he marries Rebecca, granddaughter of Nahor—Abraham's brother. Abraham dies at the age of 175. Thereafter, Rebecca conceives twins in her womb. Immediately, the two boys from the time of their birth take over the scene from Isaac. In an earlier chapter, I had mentioned that God chooses his servants in their mother's womb. The following incident proves my point. Allow me to quote an incident from Genesis 25:21-23. "Because Rebecca had no children, Isaac prayed to the Lord for her. The Lord answered his prayers, and Rebecca became pregnant. She was going to have twins, and before they were born, they struggled against each other in her womb. She said, 'Why should something like this happen to me?' So she went to ask the Lord for an answer. The Lord said to her, 'Two nations are within you; you will give birth to two rival peoples. One will be stronger than the other; the older will serve the younger.' Two nations created in a mother's womb, not by human effort or design, but by God's will!

The two boys are born. The older is named Esau because he was hairy and reddish in color—another proof that God created color of the skin, and not evolution—and the younger is named Jacob because he was born holding tightly to the heel of Esau. Next we see them as young adults. Esau, a simple hunter, carelessly sells his birthright to the sly Jacob, their mother's pet. Then we read how Rebecca and Jacob cheat blind Isaac in giving his final blessing to Jacob instead of the firstborn, Esau. Esau plans to kill Jacob, so Jacob, with the help of his mother, escapes to Mesopotamia. A strange occurrence takes place during Jacob's journey, and part of God's plan is revealed to the reader.

A tired Jacob lies down to rest and falls asleep and sees a vision at a place he names as Bethel after his dream (Genesis 28: 19). He sees a stairway reaching from heaven to the earth and angels going up and down. He sees the Lord standing beside him and renewing the promise made to Abraham. "I am the Lord of Abraham and Isaac, I will give you and your descendents this land on which you are lying. They will be as numerous as the specks of dust on the earth. They will extend their territory in all directions and through you and your descendents I will bless *all [italics mine] nations*. Remember I will be with you and protect you wherever you go and I will bring you back to this land [Promised Land]. I will not leave you until I have done all that I have promised you." What a fantastic promise! I request readers to remember this promise throughout this book.

Jacob may not have understood or grasped the depth and consequence of this promise. He may not have known until many years later that God was appointing him as the progenitor of all the Israelites. However, he sets up a memorial and, true to his nature, bargains even with God without knowing what great things are in store for him than the simple things he was asking at the moment. He says, "If you will be with me and protect me on the journey I am making, and give me food and clothing and if you return me safely to my father's home then you will be my God. This memorial will be your place of worship, and I will give you a tenth of every thing you give me." How ironic. While God is placing the world at Jacob's feet, Jacob is offering a bribe of a tenth of which God is going to give him. Humans, huh?

Here we can learn a little of God's nature. That is, many a times, God uses people unexpectedly to carry on his work. He used Abraham, a pagan, to establish his holy nation, and now we see him using Jacob, a cunning person, to further his work.

Jacob then goes to Mesopotamia, lives there for many years, marries, and has children, and when things begin to sour up between him and his father-in-law, he returns to his father's land. It is on the return journey that we understand God's full plan for all the drama in Jacob's life. At a place called Peniel (named by Jacob after the incident I am narrating now), on the bank of River Jabbok, God meets Jacob face-to-face and wrestles with him until daybreak, and since Jacob does not give up, God blesses him and anoints him with a new name, Israel. It is here that the nation of Israel was born. The passage 28 of Genesis chapter 32 is important to be read and understood. The man said, "Your name will no longer be Jacob. You have struggled with God and man and you have won, so your name will be *Israel [italics mine]*." Isn't God showing us once again that he can and will come in God-man form whenever he wants? Food for thought I must say. I don't think the word wrestle used in this passage means God had a physical combat with Jacob, but God put Jacob to some sort of severe test from which he came out successful.

God's promise to Jacob before his name was changed at Bethel, and his promise after establishing him as Israel are very important events in the history of the world because through Jacob's twelve sons and their descendents, this promise will be bestowed upon all Israelites first and then the English-speaking Christians of Europe, the British Empire, the Americas, and then the other people of the world. We will establish later how the English-speaking Christians of Europe, the British Empire, and America are connected with the promise to Jacob. As we read, we will also understand how the past and the current events and the prophecies of the prophets and Jesus are connected with this promise. This may sound ridiculous—how a promise made to one man thousands of years ago could affect the lives of every one, even to this day. Well, that is what this book is all about.

Jacob had twelve sons from four wives. Leah and Rachel were sisters, and Bilhah was Rachel's slave girl who bore children to Jacob with Rachel's permission (before Rachel had her own). Zilpah was Leah's slave girl, and she too bore children to Jacob with Leah's permission. Leah's sons were Reuben, Simeon, Levi, Judah, Issachar, and Zebulum. The sons of Rachel were Joseph and Benjamin. The sons of Bilhah, Rachel's' slave, were Dan and Nephtali, and the sons of Zilpah were Gad and Asher. These were the ancestors of the Twelve Tribes of Israel. However, the tribe of Judah was specially chosen by God to further his holy nation. How and why, we will know as we read along.

Now the scene is taken over by Joseph from Jacob. We are told that Jacob loved Joseph more than all his other sons. When Joseph was seventeen years old, his jealous brothers sold him to some Ishmaelite traders, who took Joseph to Egypt and sold him as a slave. Jacob is made to believe that a wild animal has eaten Joseph.

God's ways are unpredictable, especially with his chosen ones; Joseph is sold to Potiphar, an officer in the court of the king of Egypt. God blesses Potiphar abundantly through Joseph. Acknowledging this, Potiphar appoints Joseph as his personal servant. However, Potiphar's wife tries to seduce Joseph. Not being successful, she accuses him of attempted rape and gets Joseph in prison. But as the Bible says, the Lord was with Joseph.

It so happens that the king's wine steward and the baker offend the king, and they are put in the same prison as Joseph for a long time. The captain of the prison appoints Joseph as their servant. While in prison, the wine steward and the baker each have a dream and Joseph interprets their dream. Subsequently, the interpretations come true. The wine steward is restored back to his position and the baker is beheaded. This of course was God's plan to show to the others that God has given Joseph the gift to understand and interpret dreams. As usual, God had a specific reason for this too.

After two years, the king too has two dreams, one after the other. In the dream, he sees himself standing on the bank of River Nile when seven cows, fat and sleek, come out of the river and begin feeding on the green grass. Then he sees seven more cows, thin and bony, come out of the river and eat up the fat cows but still remain thin and bony. Then he wakes up but falls asleep again and sees another dream in which he sees seven heads of grain, full and ripe, growing on one stalk. Then he sees seven more head of grain sprouting, thin and scorched by the desert wind. The thin heads of grain swallow the full ones. These very strange dreams worry the king. So he tells his dream to all his magicians and wise men. But none of them are able to interpret the dream. Then the steward remembers Joseph and tells the king about Joseph's skill to interpret dreams. Joseph, by his God-given gift, not only interprets the dream but also offers a solution to overcome the calamities shown in the dream. He explains to the king and his officers that the two dreams mean the same thing. The seven fat cows and the seven full and ripe stalks of grains mean that God is going to give seven years of great plenty in the land of Egypt and the seven thin cows, and the seven scorched stalks of grains mean that God will send seven years of severe famine in the land of Egypt, which will ruin the country. The repetition of the dream means that "the matter is fixed by God and it will happen in the near future." Then as a solution, Joseph offers them this advice. He tells them that they should choose some men with wisdom and insight and put them in charge of the country. They should also appoint other officials to store one-fifth of the crops they would gather during the plenty period and guard it and use it only during the seven years of famine. That way, the people of Egypt will not starve during the seven years of famine. The king and the officials believe what Joseph tells them, and they like and approve the plan. The extremely pleased king appoints Joseph, a Hebrew slave, as the governor of Egypt and gives him all the power next only to himself. He also gives him an Egyptian name, Zaphenath Paneah. Amazing, I would say! The king then gets Joseph married to Asenath, the daughter of Potiphera, a priest in the city of Heliopolis (not to be mistaken to Potiphar, his ex-master).

I would urge my readers to read Abraham, Jacob, and Joseph's fantastic stories from Genesis 12 to Genesis 50. They are very engrossing and interesting.

During all these events, Jacob and his other eleven sons were still living in Canaan and its surroundings and were not aware of these developments. Once Joseph was well established, it was time for God, according to his plan, to bring Joseph and his family together. So God causes a famine in Canaan and Egypt, which lasts for seven years as seen by the king in his dream. So Jacob sends his sons to Egypt to bring food. Circumstances lead these eleven brothers into Joseph's hands. Joseph recognizes his brothers, and after a lot of drama (to enjoy the drama between Joseph and his brothers, please read chapters 41-47 in the book of Genesis), Jacob and Joseph's other brothers come and live in Egypt with the king's permission. The king gives them a separate fertile territory and treats them respectfully.

Meanwhile, Joseph has two sons, Ephraim and Manasseh, two important characters for our study.

It is time now for Jacob to die. But before that, yet another unique drama unfolds without which I believe the history of the world would have been quite different. Here too we see God's plan at work. First, Jacob calls Joseph (instead of his oldest son, Reuben) to his bedside and asks Joseph to make a solemn promise to bury him in his ancestor's land of Canaan. Joseph obliges with a vow. Second, according to Hebrew tradition, a father's final and choicest blessing naturally should go to his firstborn son. So in this case, it should have gone to Reuben. But Reuben had committed a grave sin of having intercourse with Jacob's concubine Bilhah (as good as a wife because she bore children to Jacob). Jacob, therefore, considers Reuben unworthy of his choicest blessings. Besides, Joseph had always been Jacob's favorite son. Moreover, since Joseph was living in Egypt from the time he was sold by his brothers, Jacob probably did not have an opportunity to narrate God's covenants to Joseph until then, so he wanted to divulge them before his death. Also, Jacob felt obligated to Joseph now because he was living under Joseph's care. All these reasons could have prompted Jacob to summon Joseph to his deathbed so that he could narrate the covenants (Genesis 48:3-4) and give his blessings. Joseph, however, being a great man, already may have thought that he does not need any more blessings. So he asks Jacob to bless his two sons in his place. Now see how God's providence works here. Though the boys were born to an Egyptian woman (a non-Jew), Jacob breaks a strong age-old tradition and owns Ephraim and Manasseh as his sons, not as grandsons, in place of Reuben and Simeon, his first and second born (Genesis 48:5) and immediately authenticates his acceptance by blessing the boys so that the other eleven sons, and later his descendents, would not dispute their inheritance.

Another very important drama unfolds during the time of blessing the boys. Joseph, following the tradition, places Manasseh, being the older, on the right side of Jacob and Ephraim, being the younger of the two, to Jacob's left side. But God's providence prompts Jacob to cross his hands and place his right hand on Ephraim and his left hand on Manasseh and give the blessings. Joseph gets upset of course and tries to correct his father, thinking Jacob has made a mistake because of old age and poor sight. But Jacob refuses and then reveals a truth, which has shaped and is shaping and will shape the history of the world.

Dear reader, note this carefully. While Genesis 48:13-14 shows God's involvement in action through Jacob, in Genesis 48:19-22, God prognosticates the history of the world to all people (then and now) through him. Let us note Jacob's words, "I know, son, I know. Manasseh will also become a great people [singular]; but his younger brother will become greater than he, and his descendents will become great nations [plural]." So God causes Jacob to bless the boys that day saying, "The Israelites will use your names when they pronounce blessings. They will say, may God make you like Ephraim and Manasseh." That is why Jacob put Ephraim before Manasseh. Then Jacob said to Joseph, "As you see, I am about to die, but God will be with you and will take you back to the land of your ancestors. It is you and not your brothers that I am giving Shechem, that fertile region which I took from the Amorites with my sword and my bow." Remember, the entire Israelite clan was uprooted from Canaan during the famine and were living in Egypt ever since. Thus, Jacob was predicting to Joseph that the Israelites would go back to their promised land some day, some 480 years later. The Israelites lived for 430 years in Egypt since Jacob and his sons first arrived during the famine, then they wandered 50 years in the desert during the Exodus with Moses, a total of 480 years. Jacob dies at the age of 110, but he blesses all his eleven sons before that. Subsequently, his twelve sons also die before the Exodus.

It is good to remember here that during the 480 years of Israeli absence, their land, was occupied by others, and therefore they would have to take it back from them when they returned. Unfortunately, until now they have not been able to do this because of their disobedient living. This struggle will carry on till Jesus comes back again and establishes his kingdom in Jerusalem.

By the way, who are these great people, the descendents of Manasseh and the great nations, the descendents of Ephraim? Well read on. You may be surprised when you get the answer.

Chapter II C

Post flood History: Moses

By the time Joseph and his eleven brothers and the rest of the older generation died, the Israelites had increased in great numbers in Egypt. Some time later, a king who did not know anything about Joseph and the important role he had played in Egypt came to the throne. He is disturbed by the sheer number of the Israelites and becomes doubtful of their loyalty to the throne. So he forces them into slavery. This however was bound to happen because God had warned Abraham in Genesis 15:13-14 that the Israelites would have to go through this phase of slavery of four hundred years because of their disobedience. And at the end of the four hundred years, God would rescue them and take them back to the Promised Land, the land of their ancestors.

True to his word, toward the end of four hundred years, God brings Moses on the scene in the play that God was going to stage from then on. Moses' role, as we all know, was an extremely difficult one. He had to play a dual role of governing the people and to be their spiritual leader. God knew that an ordinary person would not sustain through this ordeal. Therefore, God had to prepare him well.

Following the life of Moses, we can see two similarities, one between Abraham and Moses and the other between Noah and Moses. Let me share my thoughts with you. We know that Abraham was a pagan before God called him. The Bible tells us that Moses was born a Hebrew to Amram and Jochebed but was raised by a pagan queen as her son in her palace. Under her instructions, Moses was taught all that an Egyptian prince is supposed to know (read Exodus 2:1-10). Moses actually thought he was an Egyptian and followed the Egyptian religion and their ways until by chance he comes to know that he was a Hebrew. Again, Abraham was ordered by God to leave his birthplace and go into an unknown land far away from his clan so that God could mould Abraham into his instrument. Similarly in the case of Moses, once he realizes that he was a Hebrew, his love for them causes him to kill an Egyptian who was physically abusing a Hebrew slave. Consequently, Moses has to run to a faraway land where God moulds him too as his instrument (read Exodus 2:16a).

The similarity between Noah and Moses is that we all can accept Noah's setting foot on the earth after the flood like a new birth. God saves him in a boat made out of reeds and cement. Similarly, when Moses was a baby, the Egyptian king, out of jealousy, orders to kill all the Hebrew infants. However Moses' mother bundles him up in a basket made out of reeds and tar and let it float in the River Nile. By God's providence, the king's daughter finds Moses and takes him as her son. Thus, Moses too is saved and finds new life (read Exodus 2:1-10).

These observations are important because I believe that through these occurrences, God wants us to know that he chooses his servants in their mothers' wombs.

After killing the Egyptian, Moses flees and, after many days of journey in the desert, reaches Median. Then, under typical movie like circumstances, Moses rescues Jethro's daughter Zipporah from some unruly shepherd hands, near a common community well. A grateful Jethro hires him as his shepherd hand and allows him to stay in his household. Subsequently, Moses marries Jethro's daughter and lives a very hard life of a shepherd (Exodus 2:16b-21). God begins his process of preparing Moses for a great task.

Many years later at the proper time (at the approach of four hundred years), God calls Moses by appearing to him in a burning bush. Though the bush was burning, miraculously the fire was not consuming it. God renews his promises made to Moses' ancestors once again and tells Moses that he has chosen him to rescue the Israelites from Egyptian slavery. A fascinating dialogue is exchanged between God and the reluctant and scared Moses. But God instills courage in Moses by introducing himself as "I am who I am" and giving him divine powers. God also orders Moses and tells him to instruct all the Israelites to address him as "I am" in the future. Through this order, God declares that he is always in the present tense (omnipresent). I would urge my readers to read Exodus 3:1-22 and 4:11-17.

Moses leaves Median and goes to Egypt and, as per God's instructions, meets with Aaron, his brother, who was in Egypt all along and narrates God's instructions to Aaron and prepares him for the great task as his assistant. Then by God's command, both of them meet with the king of Egypt and request him to allow the Israelites to go three days' distance into the desert to offer a sacrifice and celebrate a festival to honor God. But God at the same time, according to his plan, the Bible tells us, makes the king stubborn and makes him reject Moses' request. Moreover, in retaliation, God makes the king give orders to further torture the Israelites (read Exodus 5:1-20). It may be difficult to understand and accept the fact that God can and does make people stubborn and do the wrong things. But God has clearly told us in Isaiah 55:8-9, "'My thoughts,' says the Lord, 'are not like yours, and my ways are different from yours. As high as the heavens are above the earth, so high are my ways and thoughts above yours.'" Through this passage, God is trying to tell us not to worry, doubt, or question his actions/decisions because he knows what is good for us.

Seeing the Israelites' plight, Moses complains to God (read Exodus 5:22-23). But God appears to Moses and encourages him and orders him and Aaron to go to the king again, this time to ask the king to release the Israelites totally from the bondage and set them free to go to their own land (read Exodus 6:1-13). The king once again refuses, and as a consequence, God sends ten terrible plagues one after another on Egypt. (For details of the disaster, read Exodus 7:14-25, chapters 8, 9, 10, 11, and 12:1-36]. In the tenth disaster, the king's and all the Egyptians firstborn sons die. The frightened king orders all the Israelites to leave the country immediately.

On the day, the 430th year ended, all the 12 tribes of the Lord's people leave Egypt (Exodus 12:37-42), about 600,000 men, not counting women and children. Thus, what God had foretold to Abraham comes true. As promised, the Israelites take the body of Jacob with them.

God is a clever God, and he knows the hearts of his people. He knew that as long as things went smooth and to their liking, the Israelites would follow Moses. But as soon as they faced any little trouble, they would rebel, curse, and try to go back. God did not want this to happen. So instead of leading them by the shorter road, by the coast of the Mediterranean Sea, he leads them by a roundabout way.

Meanwhile the king regrets his hasty action of releasing the slaves. So he pursues them. But God, through Moses, parts the Red Sea and creates a dry path at the bottom of the sea for the Israelites to cross. After all the Israelites had crossed, God causes the Egyptian soldiers to follow and, when they were in the middle of the sea, drowns them by bringing the water to its normal level (Exodus 14:1-31). Recent discoveries have documented an underwater pathway at the Gulf of Aquaba exactly at the spot where the Bible says that the Hebrews crossed the Red Sea. Chariot boxes, human skeletal remains, four-, six- and eight-spoke chariot wheels, etc., used only during the time Ramases II and Tutmoses (Moses), have also been found. I just received an e-mail with photos of giant-sized human skeletons excavated by archeologists at the site where the twelve spies sent by Moses (as per God's instruction) had encountered giant-sized human beings (read the entire chapter from the book of Numbers 13, especially 13:33). Readers may find these photos on Google under "giants of Canaan." Could these be the same giant 'Nephilims' mentioned on page 38?

But in spite of the miracle of the Red Sea, the Israelites begin complaining, and God performs more miracles by sending them manna, wafer-thin bread from heaven, and quails as meat (Exodus 16:1-35) and water from the rock at Massah and Meribha, which is still flowing (Numbers 20:1-13). Three months after they left Egypt, they reach Mount Sinai and camp there. It is at Mount Sinai that the greatest event of the Old Testament takes place.

This event would change the history of the world! It is here that the Lord hands over his plan, his law, and his Ten Commandments to the nation of Israel. These laws (613, including the Ten Commandments, mentioned in the Torah for the Jews and the Ten Commandments and the laws mentioned in the book of Leviticus in the Bible for the Christians) would be distinctly different from the laws of the pagans. Out of the 613, 365 are negative restrictions, and 248 are positive commands. Only the faithful followers of these commandments would be known as God's own people in the future. The entire promises God made to Abraham would bear fruit only by their faithfulness to these laws. Following the laws will be like following God. While handing over these laws, God shows his presence, his power, authority, and majesty through fire, clouds, thunder, and lightning. The overawed Israelites promise God to follow his statutes faithfully and serve him alone wholeheartedly.

Human beings are human beings after all, an unfaithful lot. Very soon, they forget their promise of good behavior. They sin again and evoke God's anger. So God punishes them and makes them wander in the wilderness for forty years until all the people who were twenty years and older when they left Egypt, including Moses, die in the wilderness (Deuteronomy 1:34-40)—"I have let you see it, but I will not let you go there" (Deuteronomy 34: 4). God only lets Joshua and Caleb (for their faithfulness) and those who were below twenty years when they left Egypt live and enter the Promised Land. (Please read the book of Numbers chapter 14:1-38 to know about Joshua and Caleb.)

To properly understand the evolvement of the nation of Israel, it is absolutely necessary to read the rest of the Old Testament along with the secular history. I would have liked to produce a concise form in this book, but I wouldn't be doing justice to the purpose of this book. Therefore, I would strongly urge my readers to take time and read the rest of the Old Testament. However, you may skip the book of Job, Psalms, Proverbs, Song of Songs, Ecclesiastes, and Lamentations. These books, though, will help you gain more knowledge and understanding as they did to me.

Chapter II D

Post flood History
Moses to Jesus

I assume that you have read the Old Testament as per my request and now have a good idea as to how God established the nation of Israel. However, for those who have not read, let me briefly reproduce the events.

Just before Moses dies, God asks him to appoint Joshua as the leader in his place and to appoint Caleb to assist Joshua. God blesses Joshua as he had blessed Moses, and Joshua successfully manages to get possession of the Promised Land albeit little by little. As we all know, a lot of debate has been going on over the centuries about the forceful occupation of the land—how a merciful God could allow such massacre. I really do not have an answer, but I have a theory.

We have to understand that God appointed the people of Israel as his chosen people not out of favoritism—God had always shown that all are his children—but because he had a plan to bring salvation to the world through his son Jesus. That plan needed a special race, and that race had to have its own land. This land—Bethlehem in Judah—was chosen for the birth of Jesus (Matthew 2:6). God wanted to prepare that race thoroughly to recognize and accept the Messiah when he came. That is why over the centuries, God inspired many prophets to announce the arrival of Jesus.

Again, during the 480 years of their absence, the pagans had occupied their land. Obviously, the pagans would not let the Israelites have their land back without a fight. Imagine Joshua going to all the people settled there for over four hundred years and asking them to vacate the land, and the occupants handing the land without any resistance. Also, there are many examples cited in the Bible wherein we are shown that God had allowed bad things to happen to his own people so that they could derive his blessings out of it (remember Isaiah 55:8-9). Three profound examples are the purification of heaven through war between the good angels and the bad angels, the destruction of the whole world by flood to purify the sinful human race, and then the most humiliating and excruciatingly painful death of his only begotten son, Jesus, on the cross to bring salvation to the world though he was sinless and blameless. The point is I have accepted that I cannot understand God's ways, and therefore, instead of racking my brain over the things I do not understand, I have decided to leave God's things to God and trust as good all that he has done in the past and is doing now and will do in the future in his great justice. God being the owner of the universe, has the authority to do as he pleases, and I have no right to question or judge him. Period!

After the land was occupied on both sides of the Jordan, it was divided among the eleven tribes of Jacob/Israel according to God's instruction given to Moses. The extent of the territory depended on the size of the tribe. Eight and one half of the tribes settled on the west bank, and two and one half settled on the east bank of the River Jordan. The tribe of Manasseh however was divided in two, and they were the half and half tribes that lived on either side. That makes eleven tribes. The twelfth tribe, the Levi was not assigned any territory because God had elected them as priests and as such were not to possess any land. The rest of the eleven tribes were instructed to take care of all their needs. "So, the Lord gave to Israel all the land he had promised and peace prevailed over the land" (Joshua 21:43-45).

Things remained good until Joshua and Caleb and the people who entered the land with them were alive because, having seen God's work in their lives, they somehow remained faithful and followed the statutes of the Lord to a great extent. But once the older generation died, the new generation forgot all about the good things the Lord had done for them and began sinning by worshipping Baal and Astartes of the pagans who were not driven out of the land. They even intermarried and thus evoked the wrath of the Lord, and the Lord caused the neighboring countries to constantly trouble the Israelites. This kept happening off and on for many centuries. When the Israelites turned to God, God would appoint judges (not as in judges of law) to rescue them. But when they turned away from him, they would face war and trouble again. The most widely known among the judges is Samson (of the Samson-and-Delilah fame). The last of the judges was Samuel (not the prophet). When Samuel grew old, he appointed two of his sons as judges, but they did not follow the Lord. So the people forced Samuel to appoint a king as the neighboring countries had [1 Samuel 8:4-22]. This desire and the subsequent appointments of kings were starkly against God's wish. God had designed Israel to be a free nation, governed by a person chosen and anointed by himself from among his own people. But in spite of God's warning (1 Samuel 8: 18), the Israelites elected to be ruled by a king, and monarchy came into existence. The first king was Saul followed by David, a shepherd (2 Samuel 7:8-9). The highlight of David's rule is he manages to rule the nation of Israel in peace during his reign. He desires to build a temple for the Lord, but God does not permit this. David's son Solomon succeeds the throne after David. He is renowned to be the wisest person who ever lived on this earth (1 Kings 3:10-14). Also, God allows him to build the temple, which David wanted to build (1 Kings 6:1). He is known famously for solving a very difficult case of an infant, with unusual wisdom (1 Kings 3:16-28). He also received a visit from the queen of Sheba, a very unusual and unthinkable occurrence of that period (1 Kings 10:1-10).

After the death of Solomon, the nation of Israel split into two. Rehoboam, son of Solomon, displeased the people of Israel, so the ten tribes revolted and formed the northern kingdom of Israel. They retained their name Israel but made Samaria as their capital. Only the tribe of Judah and Benjamin remained faithful to Rehoboam, son of Solomon. They formed the southern kingdom of Judah and made Jerusalem as its capital, which still exists in the history book while the other, Samaria, is no more a capital. I had mentioned earlier that the tribe of Judah was specially chosen for this reason. The reason was when the Twelve Tribes split, the two tribes were to combine to become one kingdom and retain the name Judah, and these tribes alone will be called the Jews later. Ever since this incident, up to this day, the people of the northern kingdom maintained enmity with Jews, the people of the southern kingdom of Judah (1 Kings 12:19). The Bible tells us that this incident took place not because of human action but because of the will of God. God had a distinct plan, which will unfold as we go along (1 Kings 12:21-24).

Many kings ruled over Judah in succession. This is the same with Israel too, from about the middle of the ninth century BCE until the fall of Samaria (Israel). In 721 BCE, the Assyrian king Shalmaneser led a powerful army and conquered Israel and deported all the Israelites to an area "between the Black Sea and the Caspian Sea" (2 Kings 17:1-6). This is because Hosea, the king of Israel, at that time had turned away from God and lead the people away too like his ancestors. These ten tribes never returned to the God of Israel and to their homeland, ever.

Some time later, Sennacherib, king of Assyria, tried to capture the southern kingdom of Judah too, but God saved it by sending an angel to destroy Sennaceherib's army in 701 BCE. This happened because during that time, King Hezekiah, a faithful follower of the Lord, ruled the southern kingdom. Seeing the huge army of the Assyrians, he was scared, and in his anguish and fright, he cried to the Lord. God heard his prayer and saved the kingdom for a little while. But soon after, the people of Judah too strayed away from the Lord. So King Nebuchadnezzar of Babylon conquered Judah in 604 BCE and made it part of his empire. Then he returned in 597 BCE and took the then ruling King Jehoiakim prisoner to Babylon in chains. Jehoiakim's son Jehoiachin was appointed as king of Judah. He too displeased the Lord, so God made Nebuchadnezzar return and take Jehoiachin prisoner, loot all the treasure of the temple, and completely destroy it and the kingdom. He took all the Jews (only the tribe of Judah and Benjamin, the people of the southern kingdom, were and are called Jews) into captivity and took them to Babylon (2 Chronicles

36:13-21). They remained in captivity for seventy years. So what the Lord had warned through the Prophet Jeremiah [Jeremiah 25:11 and 29:10] came true—"The land will lie desolate for seventy years, to make up for the Sabbath rest that has not been observed" (also see Leviticus 25:1-7).

During the entire existence of the northern and southern kingdoms, God sent many prophets to warn the people to return to the Lord. A few times, they responded positively, but most of the time, they rejected the Lord and faced terrible consequences.

However, God's plan was not yet fulfilled. It was only half accomplished. So in 539 BCE, King Cyrus the Great of Persia defeated king Nebuchadnezzar of Babylon. During the first year of his reign, God not only prompted Cyrus to issue a decree to free the Jews and send them back to their homeland but also to support them to rebuild the completely destroyed temple in Jerusalem (Ezra 1:11). The books of Ezra and Nehemiah narrate in detail the temple-building story. Thus, God caused the Jews (not the Israelites) to return to their homeland and settle there. These are the Jews who later spread all over the world and who still follow the Jewish statutes laid down by Moses no matter which part of the world they reside. On the other hand, the Israelites who were taken to the area of the Black Sea never returned and thus lost their identity as Israelites in the pages of history.

One of the reasons why God caused the Jews to return was because of his promise to king David—"The Lord Almighty is God over Israel for ever and you will preserve my dynasty for all time, you have revealed this to me, your servant, and have told me that you will make my descendent king" (1 Chronicles 17:23-27). Again God had promised Solomon—"Because you have deliberately broken your covenant with me, and disobeyed my commands, I promise that I will take the kingdom away from you and give it to one of your official" (Jeroboam) (1 Kings 12: 16-17). "However, for the sake of your father David I will not do this in your lifetime, but during the reign of your son [Rehoboam]. I will not take the whole kingdom away from him; instead I will leave him one tribe for the sake of my servant David and for the sake of Jerusalem the city I have made my own" (1 Kings 11:9-13). Thus, the Jews are the one tribe, and from this tribe, the final king, the king of kings, the one who will rule forever, Jesus Christ was born.

The Gospel of Matthew gives the list of the ancestors of Jesus from Abraham down to Jesus. There were fourteen generations from Abraham to David, fourteen from David to exile in Babylon, and fourteen from the exile to the birth of the Messiah, Jesus Christ. It is good to remember here that Joseph (foster father of Jesus mentioned in the lineage) is not the son of Jacob the progenitor of the Twelve Tribes of Israel, but this Joseph is the descendent of David. Also, Mary conceived Jesus, Joseph's legally wedded wife, not by physical relationship between them but miraculously through the power of God's Spirit. Therefore, Jesus was the biological child of Mary, but not a biological child of Joseph (read Luke 1:26-38). I also urge the readers to read the whole New Testament now before proceeding except the book of Revelation until later.

Chapter III

The Present: Who Are We?

Our journey has brought us from Adam to Jesus. I hope you have traveled with me with an open mind as requested at the beginning. It is now time to dwell in the present. But before we begin, we have to establish certain links. We have to know for sure who we are. Here I use the word we not in the plural meaning of the word but as in two different (distinct) groups of people. The frst group I call God's people, and the second group I call pagans.

I hereby declare by my word of honor that I am using these names not with any malice or as a discriminatory tool but only to distinguish the two groups, one from the other, for our study purpose only. I also declare that the purpose of calling the first group as God's people is not to imply that they are superior in any way to the second group, the pagans, or that God favors them more than the pagans either. In fact, history gives us many examples to show how God's people had rejected God in the past and are rejecting God even now and how God had dealt with them severely in the past and is dealing with them now.

This leads us to the question as to who God's people were in the past and who they are now. Similarly, who were the pagans in the past and who are they now?

Let us find out about the pagans first. We have already established that all the human beings of the world are brothers and sisters because we are the descendents of Noah and his family who were the only people who survived the flood. We have also established that before Nimrod, all the people worshipped one God. But Nimrod led some people to worship pagan gods and that, at the Tower of Babylon, God mixed up the languages of the people, which caused them to move further away in clans and tribes and later cover the whole world. Thus, we can say that those who followed Nimrod became pagans, and their descendents remained so.

If we follow the history carefully from ancient times, we will notice that for all civilizations from all parts of the world, religion and God (in any form) were their driving force. All the great monuments such as the temples, churches, mosques, synagogues, pagodas, and other worship places bear witness to this fact. The people established these religions out of an inherent recognition of a supreme power controlling all creation. It could be either fright or awe or both. As I mentioned earlier, these religions were handed down to generations. Some of them still exist, and some have become extinct.

God (in any form) is most just and patient. Knowing the ignorance and innocence and also their faithfulness to their own religion, God has allowed the pagans to continue with their own religion, and that is why it has flourished and will continue to flourish until God's time comes to bring them into his fold. It is imperative that God will draw all humans to himself because he has created all humans into his own image. God has been and is patient with these pagans though humans are not patient with one another's religion. This may be because we think we are superior to God. Fortunately for God, the pagans are equal to God's people.

Now let us see who are God's people. These are the people who remained faithful to Adam's God who continued to be faithful to him during Abraham's, Moses', down to Jesus' time and after Jesus, the Christians of all denominations, Jews, and Moslems. However, my belief is that the separation of two distinct people began with God's call to Abraham. Before that, the two groups' worship of their own God did not hinder their everyday life. There were wars, but these wars were more for land expansion than religion expansion. Thus, Abraham's family and those who followed him to the Promised Land and their descendents became God's (chosen) people.

We all know that the Jewish, the Christian, and the Moslem religions originated in and around Jerusalem. And therefore, it has been an important place for all three religions ever since. For Jews, it is important because it is the capital of their Promised Land, and their original and subsequent temples were built there, and their entire history revolves around that area, and the important events of its future is prophesied to take place there. For the Christians, it is important because Jesus was born and grew up in Bethlehem in the land of Judah. He preached in and around Jerusalem. He was condemned, tortured within the walls of Jerusalem, and was crucified and died and rose again from the dead just outside the city gate. The Christians also believe that Jesus will come again to establish the capital of his never-ending kingdom in Jerusalem and rule from there. By the way, my readers may know that Jesus did not physically establish the Christian institution during his life, but his Apostles established it after his death (Mark 16:14-18), and even they and their followers were not called Christians. They were known as the Followers of the Way or the Church of Believers until many years later, when St. Paul (Saul before conversion, Acts 9:1-25) and St. Barnabas went to preach to a large group of Gentiles at Antioch (Acts 11:25-26). Thus, Christians are Jewish followers of Christ and also the converted Gentiles or pagans.

During the time of the Apostles (a short while after the death of Jesus), Christianity faced terrible persecution by the Romans and literally went underground and was thought to have been totally wiped out. But it survived and rose again from its ashes and later spread as wild fire, first in the Middle Eastern region, then into Europe, and then the whole world. It is this Christian community and "the lost ten tribes of Israel" who are the ones who have been shaping the course of human history, and believe it or not, the future welfare of humanity depends totally on this community to a great extent.

For Moslems, their holiest place is Mecca in Saudi Arabia. However, Jerusalem is also an equally important place for them because Al-Aqsa Mosque also known as the Temple Mount is widely considered as the third holiest site in Islam. According to Moslem tradition, Prophet Muhammad ascended to heaven on the back of his horse, Al-Burak, at the Temple Mount after meeting with the prophets who had preceded him near the holy of holies of the Jewish people.

These three religions, though separated now, have the same main root. Therefore, at a certain point in time, God will gather them together and use them to bring all the pagans into his fold. This point in time is the end of this age when two-thirds of people of this world will be destroyed—the second big bang? Actually, sinfulness has reached such a degree that the whole world is geared up for destruction very soon. Yet God would save some people because of their faithfulness, like Noah. (Please read Matthew 24:3-44 and Daniel 12:1-3.) If we carefully read the book of Prophet Daniel and the book of Revelation (please do not read the book of Revelation now), we will find some mathematical calculations that will prove that the end of time is not too far away. In fact, we are in the last second of God's time. I will come to this topic in a different chapter later.

Continuing with the discussion, who we are, we will now try to find out what happened to the lost ten tribes of Israel. But before we do so, I want to establish to my readers that God was and is involved in the affairs of the world, sometimes directly and sometimes indirectly. To do this, we have to leave the lost ten tribes of Israel to themselves for the time being and dig into King David's life once again.

Irish history records that a coronation stone called Lia Fail together with a young princess called Tea Tephi were brought to Ireland by Prophet Jeremiah and his scribe Baruch after the fall of Judah. This princess married the son of a high king, and their descendents reigned from Tera in Ireland. Later they came to Scone in Scotland. Their family tree shows that Queen Elizabeth II is a direct descendent of Tea Tephi. How did this strange incident happen and why? To answer this, let us go back to the Bible. In 2 Samuel 7:16, God tells David through Prophet Nathan, "You will always have descendents and I will make your kingdom last forever." However, we read in 2 Kings 25:7 that king Zedekiah, the last king, a descendent of David, was taken captive to Babylon after which his eyes were put out and killed. Thus, David's descendents would seem to have been wiped out. So how did God keep his promise to David?

To understand this, we have to refer to a prophecy narrated in a parable form mentioned in symbolic language in the book of Ezekiel 17:1-6 (parables and prophecies are mostly described in symbolic form in the Bible). This prophecy was foretold many centuries before the incidents actually took place. Let me quote this parable. "The Lord spoke to me, mortal man he said, tell the Israelites a parable to let them know what I, the Sovereign Lord, am saying to them; there was a giant eagle with beautiful feathers and huge wings, spread wide. He flew to the Lebanon Mountain and broke off the top of a cedar tree, which he carried to a land of commerce and placed in a city of merchants. Then he took a young plant from the land of Israel and planted it in a fertile field, where there was always water to make it grow. The plant sprouted and became a low, wide-spreading grapevine. The branches grew upward toward the eagle, and the roots grew deep. The vine was covered with branches and leaves."

Intellectuals have interpreted this parable thus. The great eagle is none other than King Nebuchadnezzar. "He flew to the Lebanon Mountain" means that he would go to the land of Judah. "Break off the top of the cedar tree" means that he would take King Zedekiah prisoner, which he did. "Carried to a land of commerce and placed it in a city of merchants" means that Nebuchadnezzar would take King Zedekiah to Babylon and keep him in exile till he kills him. All this did happen later.

"Then he took a young plant from the land of Israel" means one of Zedekiah's children (Tea Tephi, his daughter in this case because all his sons were killed by Nebuchadnezzar), and "planted it in a fertile field where there was always water to make it grow" means that this person will be placed in a different prosperous country. "The plant sprouted and became a low, wide-spreading grapevine" means that the descendents of that person would flourish and spread in the surrounding area (which happened in the case of Tea Tephi). "The branches grew upward toward the eagle" means that there will be kings and rulers coming out of them. "And their roots grew deep" means that they will be permanently established as rulers (Queen Elizabeth II still remains a queen). Thus, history proves, and we can easily accept that part of the European people are the descendents of David who is a descendent of Jacob, who is a descendent of Abraham, who is a descendent of Noah, who is a descendent of Adam.

God prompted Prophet Amos to give this encouraging prophecy to the Jews, "A day is coming when I will restore the kingdom of David, which is like a house fallen into ruins" (Amos 9:11).

Now, though the ten tribes of Israel lost their identity and were forgotten in the pages of history as Israelites, they did not disappear from the world scene totally. They couldn't because God had made a promise to their ancestors too (remember the five covenants mentioned earlier). Besides God had prompted the same Prophet Amos to warn and encourage the Israelites, "I, the Sovereign Lord is watching the sinful kingdom of Israel, and I will destroy it from the face of this earth. But I will not destroy the descendents of Jacob."

We have seen that the Israelites were taken into exile by King Shalmaneser and settled them in the region between the Black Sea and the Caspian Sea. Prophet Esdras in his second book tells us what happened to these people [2 Esdras 13:40-46]. Let me quote this very important passage. "These are the ten tribes of Israel, who were taken away into captivity during the time of king Hoshea. King Shalmaneser of Assyria captured them and deported them to a foreign land east of Euphrates River. But the ten tribes decided not to stay in that land among the many Gentiles, so they moved further east to a country where no human beings had ever lived before. There they hoped to keep their laws [they never did], which they had failed to keep in their own country." King Shalmaneser deported the Israelites around the year 722 BCE. The Bible also tells us that these captives were settled in the cities of Medes that were in the south of Armenia. We are further told that these Israelites did not stay there for long but moved further eastward for one and a half year till they reached a no-man's-land. This would mean that they traveled toward modern Azerbaijan and then north toward the ancient USSR, near the eastern foothills of the Caucasus mountain range.

History speaks of a people called Cimmerians in this area at that point in time. To know who Cimmerians are, we have to go back to the time of King Omri of the northern kingdom of Israel (1 Kings 16:21-26).

Though he ruled only for twelve years, he established a powerful dynasty and imposed his own statutes on the people. These were followed by the subsequent kings till they were taken as captives. The Assyrians called the Israelites by Omri's name—Bit Omri (Khumri). The Babylonians called them Gimmirra (Gimiri), and Herodotus, the great geographer, called them Cimmerians. This clearly shows that the Israelites lost their original name and were later known as Cimmerians. Some Cimmerians later moved toward northern Europe, some toward Western Europe, and some traveled to the Asia Minor region.

The history of ancient France tells us that from the seventh century BCE to the fourteenth century BCE, by a series of invasions, a new wave of invaders called Kumrians spread in the Gaul region. The Greeks place these Kumrians/Kimirians in the Cimmerian area (presently called Crimea). The Romans called them Ghuls or Celts. These people spread further into modern France and into the British Isles. Further, we are told that the Persians called these settlers in the Russian plain as Sa'cea. Sa'cea is derived from Isaac, father of Jacob. There is proof to indicate that the names Saxon, Scandinavian, and Scottish originated from this name.

In short, we now know that Jacob's descendents split into two nations, the northern and southern kingdoms. First, around 722 BCE, the Assyrians captured the northern kingdom, and the Israelites were taken captives. They never came back, but spread over Europe and Asia. History further tells us that the Europeans (especially the British) colonized almost the entire world. Thus we can safely conclude that the European descendents are the descendents of the ten tribes of Israel, and we can trace them in the whole of Europe, America, Canada, Australia, New Zealand, South Africa, and elsewhere. Similarly since some of them had moved into Asia Minor, we can trace their descendents among the Asian communities as well.

On the other hand, the southern kingdom of Judah was captured after 135 odd years later and taken to Babylon. But after nearly seventy years of captivity, they returned to Jerusalem. These are the Jews, as we currently know them. Although they were in captivity for seventy years, they retained their identity and continued it after returning. So we can see that, God did keep his promise to Noah made in Genesis 9:1 and to Abraham made in

Genesis 22:15-17, and his descendents have become as numerous as the stars of heaven.

Therefore, in trying to answer the question who we are, we have discovered that both the pagans and God's people are the descendents of Noah and therefore of Adam, and that both are spread all over the world albeit as different races, religions, and colors.

At this juncture, I am prompted to mention the First Nations people of the earth, both in North America and other continents. By virtue of the above-mentioned facts, I believe it is time that everyone understands and accepts that their ancestors were the direct descendents of Noah who had spread and settled all over the world. Therefore, the current generations who are their descendents are the original settlers and are our brothers and sisters. It is also high time that the current mainstream society accepts and makes amends for their shameful acts. These include the rigorous encroachment of land and culture by our forefathers, which caused social ostracization of these innocent original settlers. Time is overdue, I must say, to give them the respect, recognition and all the rights that they richly deserve, and accept them into the main stream thereby allowing them to live in peace and harmony.

I am a supporter of their search for acceptance and their struggle to assert their rights. However, since I could not obtain much information about them, I am unable to embrace these cultures and discuss them in detail in my book.

A point to be noted here is that although the First Generation people have endured many struggles over hundreds of years, their religious practices and cultures have withstood the test of time unlike the so-called civilized world.

Chapter IV

The Present: The Rise

In the previous chapter, we saw that God faithfully kept his covenant made to Abraham. But what about his covenant made to Ephraim and Manasseh, Joseph's sons through Jacob? Let me quote Genesis 49:25-26. "It is your father's God who helps you, the Almighty God who blesses you, with blessings of rain from above, and the deep waters from beneath the ground; blessings of many cattle, and children; blessings of grain and flowers, blessings of ancient mountains, delightful things from everlasting hills. May these blessings rest on the head of Joseph, on the brow of the one set apart from his brothers." These blessings were much superior to the blessings given to Joseph's brothers (Genesis 49:2-21 and 27). Combining the blessings given to Joseph and the blessings given to Ephraim of becoming great nations (plural) and Manasseh of becoming a great nation (singular), we can see that Ephraim and Manasseh were doubly blessed to become powerful nations who will have power and control over all the other nations. Besides, they will have all the wealth of the sky, the sea, and of the earth.

Sit back and think for a while, my readers. Are we not looking at the United States of America and the British Empire during their heydays? The British would proudly boast and say that the sun does not set in the British Empire! This was true indeed.

If then we are looking at these nations, history will tell us that until the year AD 1800, there was no sign of God's promises being fulfilled among the descendents of Jacob. If we see the events chronologically in the Bible, we find that Samaria fell in 722 BCE, and Jerusalem fell in 587 BCE. Then there is a vast void until Great Britain came to world dominance from AD 1800. On the other hand, the first settlers came to Virginia (America) in the early sixteenth century. From then, a steady flow of Europeans followed. Then with the Louisiana Purchase in the AD 1800, the power and prosperity of America began increasing. So the year AD 1800 can be taken as the benchmark year for both the United States of America and the British Empire. A tiny island established the largest kingdom and acquired unimaginable wealth and possessed incomparable power. Similarly, an unknown continent (until Christopher Columbus discovered it by mistake) also became the most powerful and wealthy nation in the world. So we see that God's promise to Abraham, Isaac, and Jacob bearing fruit not through Manasseh and Ephraim, but their descendents spread throughout the world after 2,520 years (God's time).

But the question is, why did God take 2,520 years precisely to fulfill his promise? Many believers and nonbelievers of the Bible may not know this fact at all, and those who know may not have given too much attention to it. Also many may have different explanations to this fact, but not as accurate as the Bible. Now, to accept these facts of the Bible, my readers will need an open mind.

Bible readers may have noticed that seven is a significant number. God took six days for creation, and the seventh day was appointed as a rest day (later called Sabbath). There were seven churches in the province of Asia, known as the seven eras, namely, Ephesus, Smyrna, Pergamum, Thyatira, Sardis, Philadelphia, and Laodicea. There are seven seals, the seven angels with seven trumpets, the seven angels with seven plagues, etc. in the book of Revelation (all explained later). The number seven is mentioned in many other places for many other reasons in the Bible.

Now let us investigate how this number seven is connected with 2,520 years.

We are all aware of God's promise to Abraham and his descendents. It seems that when God initially gave these promises, there were no strings attached. But having noticed the misbehavior of the Israelites during the forty years in the wilderness, he seems to have changed his mind because in Leviticus 26:1-13 and elaborated more in Deuteronomy 7:12-24 and 28:1-14, we read God telling Moses to instruct the Israelites that he will keep his promise as long as they obeyed his statutes. On the other hand, in Leviticus 26:14-39, elaborated in Deuteronomy 28:22-29, we read that God warns of disaster that will strike them for disobedience.

There is a key passage in Leviticus 26:28 that is of great importance for our discussion here. It says, "Then in my anger I will turn on you and again make your punishment seven times more than before." What did God mean by this seven times more than before? Here we have to remember that this is a prophecy, and prophecy is meant for both the immediate future as well as the distant future.

So to really understand this seven times, we have to take two clues from the Bible itself. In Revelation 12:6, we read about a woman fleeing to the desert and God taking care of her for 1,260 days. Then in 12:14, we are told that these 1,260 days are three and a half years. That is, 1,260 days divided by months of thirty days is three and a half years. Seven times is twice of three and a half years, which is seven years (84 months of 30 days). 84 multiplied by 30 are equal to 2,520 days.

Scholars and biblical theologians agree that in biblical language, one day is considered (on some occasions) as one calendar year. This is because in the book of Numbers, God says to Moses that he will punish Israel for forty years, one year each for the forty days the spies spent in exploring the land of Canaan (before entering the Promised Land). I would urge my readers to read the book of Numbers 13:1-33 and 14:1-37 for a clearer understanding. Therefore, we can safely accept that God's seven times punishment mentioned three paragraphs earlier (Leviticus 26:28) were 2,520 years. This also coincides with God's word in Exodus 20:5—"I will bring punishment on those who hate me and their descendents to the third and fourth generations."

The Israelites knew that they were the chosen people. They knew very well about the blessings stored for them for a thousand generations (Exodus 20:6) for their obedience. They also knew very well the punishment they would face for their disobedience. Yet just after one generation of entering the Promised Land (till Joshua and his contemporaries were alive), they gradually, knowingly, and systematically began disobeying the Lord. Yet in his goodness, God sent judges first, then his prophets to remind and warn them. But they would not give heed to them. Ultimately, God kept his negative promise too and caused the northern and the southern kingdoms to be razed to the ground by their enemies and to be taken captive to foreign lands from where the ten tribes never returned. Only the Jews of the southern kingdom returned as we saw earlier.

What I write now may seem strange, but if we study the Old Testament carefully, we can see God's plan in this too. According to God's promise to Abraham, Isaac, and Jacob, the Israelites were never meant to occupy only the Middle East. They were meant to spread and occupy the whole world, and the whole world to be blessed through them. God may have had a nicer and easier plan to carry on this task, but because of their disobedience, he had to adhere to a tougher way. So he gave them 2,520 years to spread throughout the world, albeit without power or wealth, no sign of God's promise to Manasseh and Ephraim. In one word, nothing to brag about!

However, even though both the Israelites and the Jews may have given up hope or may have forgotten God's promise during these 2,520 years, the ever-faithful God did not forget. As soon as the 2,520 years were over, suddenly after AD 1800, God began working on his original plan. Different states in America began uniting and developed into the most wealthy and powerful United States of America. And the people of a tiny country—Britain—conquered almost the whole world and also became the world's most powerful and wealthy nation with multiple colonies. Manasseh had arrived on the world scene as a great people in the form of United States, and Ephraim had also arrived as great nations on the world scene as the British Empire (Genesis 48:19).

When I think of this, I question myself many a times, can I have any doubt about God's existence, his faithfulness in keeping his promises, his total and wholehearted involvement in the world he has created and its affairs, his graciousness and love in spite of our disobedience and wavered ways? It also raises another question in my mind, and that is if God kept his negative promises in the past, will he not keep them in the future? Will there be an Armageddon, an end of two-thirds of the people living at that time? Will Jesus Christ come again as promised and end all misery, pain, and tears?

If my readers are troubled by these questions, or your curiosity has been aroused, then read on with an open mind to know the truth.

Chapter V

The Present: Fall

By the above argument, we now know that many of the people of Europe, Russia, United States, Canada, South Africa, Australia, and New Zealand are the descendents of the ten tribes of Israel. We also know that after the death and resurrection of Jesus, Christianity spread as wild fire in the Middle East, the Mediterranean region, and then on to Europe, Russia, and to other parts of the world mentioned above.

So it is arguably acceptable that the Israelites (not the Jews) settled in these areas adorned Christianity, and therefore, the Christians residing in all these areas are the descendents of the lost ten tribes of Israel.

I can visualize hairs standing and faces blushing with anger and disagreement.

Why is this identification important to our discussion? Also, why do I believe that it is true beyond any doubt?

Let us look at the world situation now (the year 2010). As I am writing, the American economy is in shambles. A country, which was handing out charity to the whole world, is almost on its knees. And if the trend continues for long, it will be seeking charity from others very soon. Very tragic indeed!!

Until 1947, the great British Empire basked in its power and might and got intoxicated with the wealth it acquired albeit forcefully and with deceit from its colonies. Now once again it is a small country that it was before. Tragic, very tragic indeed!!

Let us go to the Middle East where the Jews settled down in and around Jerusalem after returning from exile. History tells us that they too have faced innumerable hardship all along, and this hardship seems to be getting worse after they were resettled in their present location after the Second World War. If we believe that God gave that land to Abraham, then I believe that their present location is their own land. Then why are they facing these seemingly insurmountable problems? Simple answer is they were and are not sincere in following the God of their ancestors. They follow the letter, and not the spirit, of the teachings given to them. Besides, they have refused to accept that Jesus is the Son of God, the promised Messiah, up until now.

I have given only a gist of the current situation of the state of affairs of the Twelve Tribes of Jacob. For more details, my readers will have to dig into relevant history books.

The title of this chapter is "Fall." Is it not obvious that Manasseh and Ephraim have fallen flat on their nose from their pedestal as their ancestors previously had? We cannot deny that God kept his promise a hundred percent, so what happened?

It seems that we human beings never learn from our mistakes. This, however, is not entirely our fault, I must say (if it is any consolation). God created human beings in his own image, like himself in all ways except his godliness (creative superiority). In fact, he created Adam and Eve with immortality until they disobeyed and brought mortality into existence. But at the same time, he gave them free will and choice. Planting the Tree of Life and Knowledge in the middle of the Garden of Eden and telling them not to eat only from those trees is proof of this. Adam and Eve, on their own, would never have eaten the fruit, I am sure, simply because sin and evil was not in them. However, the deceitful, jealous, and scared (of losing dominion over the earth) Evil One deceived these two innocent people (he does the same even now). The Evil One could do this quite easily because he was an angel who became Satan whose power was not taken away by God. He used this deceitful power, and Adam and Eve easily fell for his trick and disobeyed God. Thus, sin and death came into the world. We can see this trait in human beings, raising its ugly head every now and then throughout history. This is true even now, especially when things are going on very well. Human beings forget God and start behaving like gods themselves.

What happened to the British Empire is happening to the United States of America right now. The wealth of the sky, sea, and the land and incomparable power was showered abundantly on them, and this has bloated their heads with ego. They have totally forgotten where it came from. Their pride and vanity (like Satan's) in their advancement in all fields is making them believe that they have ultimately arrived and that there is no God or there is no need of him anymore. Thus, they are systematically neglecting God and are gradually but surely drifting away from him. Christianity, with all its denominations, is currently the predominant religion in the world, but this is only for name's sake. Their faith has become superficial. There is enough proof that majority of the Christians do not own a Bible, read, or study it, and therefore do not actually know what it contains. Some acknowledge it only as a myth or nice story to be read once and forgotten. Thus, in one word, majority of the Christians have abandoned God totally in about two hundred years (as was after Joshua and Caleb). The consequence is the current chaotic situation of the world in different forms. Once again, we can see Bible prophecy coming true gradually. Though God is warning us repeatedly in various ways (devastating earthquakes in Haiti and Chile in one month's time), the ruler of this world, the great deceiver as always has managed to win over us (as he did over Adam and Eve). He is making us believe that we have all the power, the wealth, the knowledge, and the time to overcome these calamities by ourselves. He is subtly obstructing us in reading and knowing the Word of God lest our minds are enlightened and our eyes are opened and we can see clearly the signs of impending catastrophe hovering over our heads. He is desperately trying to devour every one without even our knowing it because he knows that his time is almost over. He most surely knows that the world is at the last quarter of the last minute of the sixth era, and very soon Jesus will come, and his dominion will be overthrown, and he will be cast away in the abyss (not hell) for a thousand years (more of this later).

Although we have been noticing this trend for quite some time now, we have not only been showing lack of responsibility but also pacifying/consoling ourselves by giving all sorts of explanations and excuses. In our foolishness caused by the Evil One, we are stubbornly refusing to accept the fact that we are happily marching toward impending disaster (as during the time of Noah). I sincerely hope that this recession, the earthquakes, the constantly recurring floods and tsunamis, the out-of-control calamities, the wars, terrorism, so on and so forth, will open our eyes and minds to see the steep downward slide we are in, which is taking us to the final fall. Unless we acknowledge our detachment from God, ask for forgiveness, and turn to him soon, our ultimate doom is inevitable and soon too. May God alone help us all!! With the word us here, I am addressing people of all religions.

My readers would do well to consider seriously the Bible passage I am going to reproduce below, (Ezekiel 7:1-5 and 10-14).

> The Lord spoke to me, "Mortal man, this is what I, the Sovereign Lord, am saying to the land of Israel (the Twelve Tribes of Jacob and, therefore, to the white Christian people spread all over the world, mentioned earlier and through them to all the people). This is the end for the whole land! Israel, the end has come. You will feel my anger, because I am judging you for what you have done. I will pay you back for all your disgusting conduct. I will not spare you or show you any mercy. I am going to punish you for the disgusting things you have done, so that you will know that I am the Lord."
>
> This is what the Sovereign Lord is saying, "One disaster after another is coming on you. It is all over. The end is coming for you people who live in the land. The time is near when there will be no more celebration, only confusion on the mountain shrines." (Ezekiel 7:1-5)
>
> Mountain means "country" in the Bible.

> The day of disaster is coming, violence is flourishing. Pride is at its height. Violence produces more wickedness. Nothing of theirs will remain, nothing of their wealth, their splendor, or their glory. The time is coming, the day is near when buying and selling will have no more meaning, because God's punishment will fall on every one alike. No merchant will live long enough to get back to what he has lost, because God's anger is on every one. Those who are evil cannot survive. The trumpet blows, and everyone begins to get ready. But no one goes off to war [no one can because war and destruction will be all around], for God's anger will fall on everyone alike. (Ezekiel 7:10-14)

Ezekiel's prophecy is upheld by Jesus in different words in the Gospel of Luke 21:20 wherein Jesus tells his disciples, "When you see Jerusalem surrounded by armies, then you will know that she will soon be destroyed." Was Jesus talking only about the destruction of Jerusalem, which occurred shortly after his death? I don't believe so because in the book of Revelation 16:14, we read, "These three spirits go out to all the kings of the world, to bring them together for battle on the day of the Almighty God." Revelation 16:16 further confirms, "Then the spirit brought the kings together in the place that in Hebrew is called Armageddon." At the battle of Armageddon, near Jerusalem two thirds of the population will be destroyed (more about this later).

A note to the readers, in Revelation 18, the fall of Babylon is mentioned. Readers have to understand that this Babylon is the future Jerusalem because the current Jerusalem will be destroyed once again like the ancient Babylon.

As I am writing this book, I just received an e-mail, which I think fits well with what I have written.

> Lucia reveals the Third Secret of Fatima
>
> Independently of any Creed or Religion, it is better to be prepared and be in good terms with God though we never know when we will be leaving this world.

Last Secret of Fatima

The church has given permission to reveal to the people the last part of the message. The Blessed Virgin appeared to three children in Farina, Portugal, in 1917. This is a proven fact; one of these children is still alive. Her name is Lucia. She is a cloistered nun and lives in a monastery in Portugal.

Lucia disclosed the message for the first time to Pope Pius XII who, after reading it, sealed it and stored away without making it public. Later Pope John XXIII read it and, in the same manner as his predecessor, kept it out of the public eye because he knew that once revealed, it will bring desperation and panic to humankind.

Now the time [end time] has come, and permission has been granted from Pope John Paul II to reveal it to the children of God in order not to create panic but to make people aware of this important message so everybody can be prepared. The Virgin Mary told Lucia: "Go, my child, and tell the world what will come to pass during the 1950s-2000s. Men are not practicing the Commandments that our Father has given us. Evil is governing the world and is harvesting hate and resentment all over. Men will fabricate mortal weapons that will destroy the world in minutes; half of the human race will be destroyed [Armageddon?]. The war will begin *against Rome* [italics mine], and there will be conflicts amongst religious orders.

God will allow all natural phenomena like smoke [volcanic eruption in Iceland?], hail, cold, water, fire, floods, earthquakes, winds and inclement weather to slowly batter the planet. "Those who won't believe, this is the time to change. Those lacking charity toward others and those who do not love their neighbours like my beloved Son has loved you, cannot survive. They will wish they had died. Our Lord God will punish severely those who do not believe in him, those who despise him and those who did or do not have time for him.

"I call upon all of you to come to my Son Jesus Christ, God helps the world, but all of those who do not show fidelity and loyalty will be destroyed."

Father Agustin, who lives in Farina, said that Pope Paul VI gave him permission to visit Sister Lucia who is a cloistered nun (she does not leave the monastery nor is allowed to receive any visitors). Father Agustin said that she received him greatly overwhelmed and told him, "Father, Our Lady is very sad because nobody is interested in her prophecy of 1917. Though the righteous are walking through a narrow path, the evil ones are walking through an ample road that is leading them straight to their destruction. Believe me, Father, the punishment will come very soon.

"Many souls will be lost. Many nations will disappear from the earth. But in the middle of all these, if men reflect, pray, and practice good deeds, the world can be saved. But if men persist with its evil, the world will be lost forever.

"The time has come for all to pass on the message of our Blessed Lady to their families, friends, and to the entire world. Start praying, to make penitence and sacrifices. *We are at the last minute of the last day* [italics mine] and the catastrophes are near. Due to this, many that were far from the church will return to the open arms of the church of Jesus Christ [during tribulation]. England, Europe, Russia, America, China, and all other nations, Jews, Muslims Christians of all denomination, and people of other religions will join and become One, Holy, Catholic, and Apostolic Church. All will return believing and worshipping God our creator, in his beloved Son, and in our Blessed Mother Virgin Mary."

What awaits us?

Everywhere there will be peace talks, but there will be no peace. Instead a man in a very important position will be assassinated, and this will provoke the war. A powerful army will dominate all through Europe, and the nuclear war will commence.

This war will destroy everything. Darkness will fall over us for seventy-two hours [three days] and the one-third of humanity that survives this obscurity and sacrifice will commence to live a new era. They will be good people. In a very cold night, ten minutes before midnight, a great quake will shake the earth for eight hours. This will be the third signal from God to show that he is the one who governs the earth. But the righteous and those who propagate the faith and the message of the Lady of Fatima need not fear.

"What to do? Bow your heads, kneel down, and ask God for forgiveness because only what is good and is not under the power of evil will survive the catastrophe. In order for you to prepare and remain alive, I will give you the following signs: Anguish. And in a short period, the earthquake will commence. The earth will shake. The shake will be so violent that it will move the earth twenty-three degrees, and it will return it to its normal position. Then total and absolute darkness will cover the entire planet. Satan and his demons will freely mingle around, doing harm to all those people that did not want to listen to this message and those who did not want to repent.

"The faithful people, remember to light the blessed candles, prepare a sacred altar with a crucifix in order to communicate with God and implore for his infinite mercy. All will be dark. In the sky, a great mystic cross will appear to remind us the price that his beloved Son had to pay for our redemption.

In the house, the only thing that can give light will be the holy candles. Once lit, nothing will put them off until the three days of darkness are over. Also, you should have holy water that should be sprinkled abundantly on windows and doors. The Lord will protect the people inside and the property of the chosen ones [as what happened during the Passover in Egypt—read Exodus 12: 7 and 13].

"Kneel down before the powerful cross of my beloved Son, pray the Rosary, and after each Hail Mary, you must pray the following: "Oh, God, forgive us our sins. Preserve us from the fire of hell. Take all souls to heaven, especially those who are in more need of thy mercy. Blessed Virgin Mary, protect us. We love you. Save us and save the world."

"Pray five [Apostles'] Creeds and the Rosary, which is the secret to my Immaculate Heart. All those who believe in my words, go and take the message to everyone. Talk to all the people now that there is time, for those who keep quiet will be responsible for all those people who will perish in ignorance. All those who pray humbly the rosary, fear nothing during the Lord's Great Day for you will have the protection of heaven. But those who are bound to die, I will help them die in peace, and they will be holy when they enter the other world. I exhort all my children to attend Mass every first Friday and every first Saturday of each month to confess and receive Holy Communion, and in doing so, save the world from its total destruction."

When the earth shakes no more, those who still do not believe in our Lord will perish in a horrible way. The wind will bring gas, and it will disperse it everywhere, then the sun will rise. Maybe you will survive this catastrophe.

Do not forget that God's punishment is holy, and once it has started, you should not look outside under no circumstance. God does not want any of his children to see when he punishes the sinners [Exodus 12:12-13]. All this encompasses with the writings of the Holy Scriptures. Read on the New Testament: Luke 21:5-12, 12:19, 20:20, 29:33, Letters of St. Paul 3:8-14, Isaiah 40, and 1:5-9. You must understand that God allows all this to happen. The pope and bishops are now awaiting another message that speaks about repentance and prayer. Remember that God's words are not a threat, but good news. Please reproduce these pages and send them to all you know so we all can have the opportunity to repent and be saved. We do not know if those receiving this message believers or are non-believers in God, but think that if you are receiving this message, it is for a reason!

The Creator is giving us the chance to be saved no matter what *religion or creed* [italics mine] you belong. If you don't believe in this message, at least send it to others. It costs you nothing. To all those who receive it, they will have the opportunity to judge for themselves. Remember, we can avoid a great deal if we practice the Commandments that our Father God left us. The Ten Commandments are ten simple things, that if we all put in practice, we can obtain God's pardon.

Please Note:
Can we be naive enough to ignore these warnings? We better not if we awaken ourselves and look around.

The word anger mentioned in the passages above should be taken as regret (sorrow) and disappointment of God, parallel to the passage in Genesis 6:5-8, and not as in vengeance.

Chapter VI

Transition—Past to Present: First Proof

At the end of the last chapter, I had mentioned that the spirit would bring the (evil) kings together at a place that in Hebrew is the Armageddon. These kings will fight with each other in a battle called the Battle of Armageddon. This clearly shows that Armageddon is not the name of the event, but it is the name of the place. However, in the book of Revelation, an even more appropriate name is given to this battle, "the battle on the great day of Almighty God" (Revelation 16:14). So where is this place? Before going there, we have to understand that these spirits mentioned earlier are not God's spirits (angels) but evil spirits of Satan because it is clearly mentioned in the book of Revelation 16:13-14 that, "Then I saw three unclean spirits that looked like frogs. They were coming out of the mouth of the dragon, the mouth of the beast and the mouth of false prophet [all three are Satan's agents]. These are the spirits of demons that will perform miracles [actual miracles to deceive people]. These three spirits will go out to all the evil kings of the world to bring them together."

These kings and spirits will fight with Jesus' army. This is described in three places in the Bible. In Revelation 19:11, we read, "Then I saw heaven open, and there was a white horse. Its rider is called Faithful and True. It is with justice that he judges and fights his battles." In Revelation 19:13, we read, "He wore a robe that was covered with blood. His name is the Word of God." Then again in Revelation 19:16, we read, "On the robe and on his thigh was written his name; King of Kings and Lord of Lords." Again Revelation 19:19-21 says, "And then I saw the beast [Antichrist] and the [evil] kings of the earth and their armies gathered together to fight against the One who was riding the horse and against his armies. The beast was taken prisoner together with the false prophet who had performed miracles. The beast and the false prophet were both thrown alive into the lake of fire that burns with sulphur. Their armies were killed by the sword that came out of the mouth of the One who was riding the horse." Revelation 20:1-3 continues, "Then I saw an Angel coming down from heaven, holding in his hand the key of the abyss [not hell] and a heavy chain. He seized the dragon, that ancient serpent [the one who deceived Adam and Eve], that is the devil or Satan, and chained him up for a thousand years. The Angel threw him in the abyss [not hell], locked it, and sealed it, so that he could not deceive the nations any more until the thousand years of Jesus' reign was over. After that he [the devil] must be let loose for a little while." Why? This important truth will be revealed later in this book.

So now we know that at the battle of Armageddon, Jesus will physically come down from the clouds as he did when went up (read Acts of the Apostles 1:11 especially 1:10 and Mark 16:19) and join his worldly army (his faithful ones), and fight with the armies of the Evil One. The armies of the Evil One will be defeated, and the devil that had caused all the chaos since the time of Adam will be locked up for a thousand years.

So where is this Armageddon, the place of the third and final world war? Armageddon is Har Megiddo—Hill of Megiddo in Hebrew. It is in Israel, about fifty odd miles north of Jerusalem. The entire valley of Jezreel where some major ancient battles had taken place can be seen from this hill. As recently as the First World War, the British defeated the Turkish army at the Battle of Megiddo. Why will the final battle take place only at Megiddo, and not anywhere else in the world? For two reasons, I would think. First, because when Jesus was taken to heaven from the Mount of Olives and the Apostles were still looking at the sky, they had received a solid promise that Jesus will come back again at the same spot (Acts 1:10-11), mentioned earlier. So that is where Jesus will gather his army for the battle. Second, Jerusalem has been the center of all activities from the time Abraham settled down there, so it is but inevitable that the end should come from there.

A logical question may arise in my readers' mind, and a fair one I would say. That is, how can we be sure that the event of Armageddon will surely take place and very soon? In short, how can we trust that the Bible prophecy will come true? The first part I will try to answer now, but the second part, I will have to answer later as it will make a chapter of its own.

We have to remember here that the people of this world have been wrestling to believe the truth mentioned in the Bible ever since. That is because the people do not know the truth that the Bible interprets itself. To know and understand these interpretations, it takes a lot of patience, careful reading and studying, and the guidance of an unbiased guide. But most importantly, the wisdom of the Holy Spirit that comes gradually with commitment. Also, because the Bible has been interpreted in so many different ways, it is difficult, if not impossible, to know which one is the right one. Even my interpretation will be an added one to the many existing already. But since my work is not theologically based, and all I am trying to do as mentioned right at the beginning of this book is to reproduce the simple understanding that I have acquired from my numerous readings to the simple-minded people, I am satisfied that this book will not brew division.

From this point on, I will be narrating a story, and I hope my readers would not mind. However, this is not an old woman's bedtime story but the fact of history. At this point, I would strongly urge my readers to read the entire book of Daniel for a much better understanding. The book of Daniel was written between 618 BCE and 536 BCE. The book is amazing.

Let us step back into history to the time of King Nebuchadnezzar around 604 BCE. He had captured the city of Jerusalem and razed it to the ground and taken the Jews prisoners to Babylon. After a little while he had ordered Ashpenaz, his chief officer, to select some young men from among the exiles to be trained for three years, at the end of which they would be required to serve the king. They were to be taught all the Babylonian ways including their language. Daniel and his three friends, Hannniah, Mishael, and Azariah, among others, were chosen. After three years of successful training, Daniel and his three friends were inducted into the royal court because they had highly impressed the king and his authorities with their wisdom. God had blessed them with so much wisdom that they outsmarted all the magicians and fortune-tellers of the kingdom. Daniel remained in the royal court until Cyrus, the emperor of Persia, conquered Babylon around 539 BCE.

In the second year that Nebuchadnezzar was king, he had a dream (Daniel recorded it in the year 550 BCE, so the dream must have occurred that year). This strange dream worried the king so much that he called all his fortune-tellers and magicians not only to reveal the dream on their own but also to interpret it. The fortune-tellers, the magicians, and the wizards could not meet the king's demands, so the king ordered their execution.

Daniel, however, through God's providence, managed to send word to the king that he is able to interpret his dream. So the king called him and asked him if he could really do what he says. So Daniel said these famous words, "Your Majesty, there is no wizard, magician, fortune-teller or astronomer who can do that. But there is a God in heaven that reveals mysteries. He has informed your majesty what will happen in the future, now I will tell you your dream" (Daniel 2:27-28).

> In this dream the king had seen a giant statue standing, bright and shining and terrifying to look at. Its head was made of fine gold; its chest and arms were made of silver; its waist and hips were made of bronze; its legs of iron and its feet partly of iron and partly of clay. While the king was looking at it, a great stone broke loose from a cliff without any one touching it, struck [only] the iron and clay feet of the statue and shattered them. At once the entire statue crumbled and became like dust on a thrashing place in summer. The wind carried it all away, leaving not a trace. But the stone grew to be a mountain that covered the whole earth! (The kings dream/vision, Daniel 2:31-49)

"Your Majesty, you are the greatest of all kings [until then]. The Lord of heaven has made you Emperor and given you power, might and honor. You are the head of pure gold. After you there will be another [second] empire, not as great as yours [silver], after that the third empire [bronze], then a fourth [iron]. Only one Emperor will rule each of these empires at a time. But the partly iron and partly clay feet means a divided empire. The partly iron and partly clay toes means that, part of the empire will be strong and part will be weak. You also saw that the iron was mixed with clay. This means that, the rulers of the empire will try to unite their families by inter marriages, but they will not be able to, any more than iron can mix with clay. Then you saw a great stone falling from a cliff without any one touching it and crushing the toes and then the whole statue crumbling to dust, and the stone itself growing into a big mountain covering the whole world. That means that, during the time of half strong and half weak empire, God of heaven will establish his Kingdom on earth that will never end. It will never be conquered but will destroy all the empires and last forever [Revelation 19:11-21 and 20:1-3]. (Daniel's interpretation)

The king believed Daniel and rewarded him by putting him in charge of the province of Babylon. Please remember this interpretation throughout the rest of the book.

Is this dream just an ordinary dream exaggerated out of proportion or really a forewarning from God? Did these incidents ever come to pass? To answer these questions, let us look at another mind-blowing incident that only Daniel could interpret.

In 539 BCE, the Persian army of Cyrus the Great was trying to conquer the city of Babylon but was unsuccessful until then. Therefore, King Belshazzar (Nebuchadnezzar's son) had thrown a banquet to celebrate the great power and invincibility of his empire. He had invited one thousand noblemen for the banquet. Suddenly, a human hand appeared from nowhere and inscribed on the wall, "Mene, Mene, Tekel, Parsin."

The Chaldeans present there understood the meaning of the terms as for weight and units, but they could not understand what they implied. Everyone was flabbergasted and did not know what to do. Even the king's magicians and astrologers could not decipher the writing. The queen mother, having heard what had happened, came to the king and told him that Daniel is the only one who could interpret the meaning (she probably was present when Daniel had interpreted her husband Nebuchadnezzar's dream mentioned earlier).

Daniel who was by then advanced in age was brought to the banquet hall. An interesting dialogue takes place between the king and Daniel (readers are encouraged to read this very important dialogue from Daniel 5:1-31). Finally, Daniel tells the king the meaning of the writing on the wall. "Number, number, weight, division." Number means "God has numbered the days of your kingdom and has brought it to an end." Weight means "you have been weighed and found to be too light" (wanting in character and faith). Division means "your kingdom will be divided and given to the Medes and Persians."

The Bible tells us and history corroborates that the same night, Darius the Mede ordered his army to divert the river that was flowing beneath the city wall and dig a canal on the dry riverbed under the massive walls. Then his army crossed over through it, opened the city gates, and let their troops enter the city and conquer it within hours. They executed King Belshazzar the same night. Thus Daniel's interpretation came true once again.

With the death of King Nebuchadnezzar and his son Belshazzar, the Babylonian Empire (the golden head of the statue) was destroyed. Then came the empire of the Medes and the empire of the Persians (the chest and shoulder of silver of the statue), which lasted for a little over two hundred years.

In 331 BCE, the Persian Empire collapsed under the powerful army of Alexander the Great, and the third empire (of bronze waist and hips of the statue) was established. However, Alexander died only a little while later, and his empire was divided among his four generals. Yet it remained Hellenistic for about three hundred years (Daniel 8:21-22).

With the above proof, we know that until now Nebuchadnezzar's dream and Daniel's interpretation had come true. In 331 BCE, the Roman Empire (the waist and legs of iron of the statue) arrived by consuming Alexander's four generals. This empire will continue almost till the end time in various forms. However, in 286 BCE, Emperor Diocletian divided the vast Roman Empire into east and west for the purpose of proper administration. Thus, the body of the statue (a single empire under various emperors) became the two legs of iron of the statue (31 BCE to AD 476). Christianity was declared as the official Roman religion by Constantinople in AD 324.

Let us now see how these two long legs have survived so far (the length of the legs depicts the lengthy time period of its survival). History tells that the Western Roman Empire was sacked and looted by Alaric and his Visigoths in AD 409. Thus, Rome received its first deadly wound in eight centuries. The mention of this deadly wound received by the beast (Rome) is mentioned symbolically in Revelation 13:3. Subsequently, three invaders—the Vandals [AD 429-533), the Heruri (AD 476-493), and the Ostrogoths (AD 493-554) ruled the western part of the Roman Empire in succession. However, the Eastern Roman Empire remained strong during this period, and they officially recognized the three western kingdoms as a continuation of Roman government. But due to negligence of the eastern emperors, the western Roman kingdoms became weaker, and they did not last long. In AD 553., the Eastern Roman Emperor Justinian conquered the Western Roman Empire and united the east and the west and formed one empire again. Thus, after seventy-seven years, the deadly wound of the Roman Empire was healed (Revelation 13:3). But Justinian had a problem as to how he would manage such a vast empire. He hit upon a brilliant idea. As the Western Empire was getting weaker, a ruler of a different kind, the bishop of Rome (the Pope) was gaining religious, civil, and political power. So Justinian made an alliance with the pope in AD 554 and thus restored the unity of the Eastern and Western Roman Empires. This restoration is known as the Imperial Restoration. Yet the emperors of the west remained as puppets in the hands of the popes who wielded total power on the west from AD 554 to

800. As years passed by, Bishop Leo became the chief pontiff. Dissatisfied with the security and protection provided by the weakening Eastern Emperors he held secret negotiations with Charles (Charlemagne), king of France, and subsequently anointed him as the emperor of Western Roman Empire. This caused displeasure to the eastern Roman emperor. However, after a few years, the eastern emperor recognized Charlemagne as coemperor.

Once again, the Western Roman Empire began disintegrating slowly under the successive rulers. Around AD 936, the Magyars were trying to invade the weak western Europe. But Otto, the king of Saxons (Germany) fought with them and defeated them in AD 955. Many years later, Pope John XII managed to convince Otto to capture Italy, and in AD 962, the latter was crowned as king.

Otto's empire survived for three hundred years, and in AD 1294, after King Conrad's death, a 199 years of kingless period resulted due to rival faction. In 1273, Rudolph I from the Hapsburg family was inducted as emperor for the imperial throne. Pope Clement VI crowned Rudolph's descendent Charles V in 1530. After Charles V, the Hapsburg family's power dwindled, and by the eighteenth century, the Roman Empire began losing its grip over Europe. The French Revolution brought Napoleon to power. He began negotiating with Pope Pius VII and was appointed as emperor two years later. Under Napoleon's pressure, sixteen princes withdrew from the Roman Empire and asked Napoleon to form a confederation and include them as part of his empire. This led Francis II, the only remaining Roman Emperor, to withdraw his title.

Napoleon's empire lasted until 1814 when a British-led coalition defeated him. Then for the next fifty years, Italy and Germany remained divided into small states. In 1871, Bismarck managed to unite Germany, and Garibaldi united Italy. In 1922, Benito Mussolini came to power and restored the ancient Roman Empire. In 1929, Mussolini signed a treaty with the pope by which the pope officially recognized the Italian government and established sovereignty over the Vatican City. Four years later, the pope signed a treaty with Hitler. Russians then entered into an agreement with Hitler, which we all know led to the Second World War.

Up until now, we have been focusing mostly on the western part of the Roman Empire (one leg). Let us now, look at the eastern part (the other leg). From AD 286, when Emperor Diocletian divided Rome, various emperors ruled the Eastern Roman Empire. One among them was Emperor Constantinople. In AD 1453, the Turks captured the city and killed Constantine, the last Greek emperor to rule the Empire. The eastern leg survived however because the pope appointed the niece of Constantine as the heir to the eastern empire and got her married to Ivan the Great of Russia. This marriage established the Russian rule to continue as successors of the Roman emperors. Thus the eastern leg continued under Russian rulers down history.

We started from the head of Nebuchadnezzar's statue in the dream, and we have reached the feet until now. So let us see what happened to the ten toes. The Bible warns us that very soon ten kings—toes of Nebuchadnezzar's statue, people with the highest authority, the successors of the eastern and western legs, will unite and try to revive the Roman Empire once again (last time). They will support a powerful ruler who will come on the world scene (mentioned in the e-mail). This ruler (Satan's representative) will dominate the whole world with deceit and almost supernatural talents. He will rule for forty-two months of thirty days, initially with peace and prosperity. Then all of a sudden, he will plunge the world into unprecedented chaos and misery, into Armageddon—the Third World War, in which two-thirds of humanity will perish. This battle, as I mentioned earlier, will be fought between the army of the Beast (Satan's representatives) and Jesus's army. Jesus will destroy Satan's army and physically rule this world for a thousand years (Revelation 12:7-17, Matthew 24:21, and 29:31).

My readers may be inclined to believe as true all what I have written until World War II, considering historical evidence. But to believe that there will be a World War III (Armageddon) and Jesus coming physically once again and fighting, winning, and ruling for a thousand years will be difficult, if not impossible, to believe. Fortunately, the Bible has enough proof about this fact, and a person with an open mind will be able to believe it quite easily. Daniel 12:9-13 says, "You must go now, Daniel, because these words are to be kept secret and hidden until the end comes.

Many people will be purified. Those who are wicked will not understand but will go on being wicked. Only those who are wise [open minded] will understand. And you, Daniel, be faithful till the end. Then you will die, but will rise [like Jesus] to receive your reward at the end of time." Remember, Daniel's prophecy was for the future, and most of it has so far come true.

Before we dig into the Bible for proof, let us take a careful look around our world. The wars that are currently going on and the constant threat of major wars hovering over humans, terrorism, the greed to grab the natural resources and the resultant chaos, earthquakes, cyclones, floods, man-eat-man attitude for survival, power, and success. Total collapse of morals and family structure, freedom for abortion, law against teaching religion in some schools and elsewhere, and now to top it all, economic collapse of the mighty and powerful nations due to selfishness and mismanagement by one most powerful country that has plunged the whole world into unprecedented pain, suffering, and misery. All these things, mind you, are prophesied in the Bible. Unfortunately, we do not read this guidebook handed down to us from centuries, and many among those who read it ignore it as all bull. And those few who believe and want to do something are helpless for many reasons.

The question here is after reading this book, can one ignore the signs at all?

The Bible tells us that the Roman Empire (depicted as the beast with seven heads in the book of Revelation 17:9-10 and also as seven hills) will be revived seven times throughout history. Let me quote it here. "This calls for wisdom and understanding. The seven heads are seven hills, on which the woman [woman means the church in the Bible] sits. They are also seven kings; five of them are fallen [by the time John saw the vision]. One still rules, [during and after John's time], and the other one has not yet come; when he comes, he must rule only a little while" (Satan's final seven years of rule, explained later.) Then Revelation 17:12 continues, "The ten horns [Revelation 17: 3c] you saw are ten kings [mentioned earlier] who have not yet begun to rule, but who will be given authority to rule as kings for one hour [short time] with the beast. These ten have only one purpose and that is to give their power and authority to the beast. They will fight against the Lamb; but the Lamb together with his called, chosen, and faithful followers, will defeat them because he is Lord of Lords and King of Kings." This simply means that the seventh head (the powerful ruler) will make a truce with a powerful European civil power consisting of ten rulers (men with ultimate authority) or ten states. Under his leadership, he will dominate the world and go into the battle of Armageddon.

The passage of Revelation 17:11, which is between the passages 10 and 12 mentioned above, is a little tricky to understand—"And the beast that was once alive, but lives no longer, is itself an eighth king who is one of the seven and is going off to be destroyed." What John is telling us here is that the Roman Empire that existed during his time will cease to exist temporarily but will be revived by the Antichrist in collaboration with Satan for the seventh and last time, which will end with the battle of Armageddon. This will be the end of the six thousand years of the world order. However, Satan's kingdom (without human collaboration) will be revived for the eighth time after Jesus' thousand years of rule. This last and final rule of Satan is believed to last for a hundred years (explained later).

Let us compare the above passage of Revelation 12:9-10 with history. The first restoration (head) occurred in AD 554 when Justinian united the divided Eastern and Western Roman Empires (after Alexander the Great). The second restoration (head) occurred when Charlemagne, king of France, was appointed as a co emperor of the weak Western Roman Empire in AD 800. The third restoration (head) occurred when Otto, German-Saxon king, was crowned in AD 962. The fourth restoration (head) occurred three hundred years later when king Rudolph's descendent Charles V was crowned Emperor in 1530. The fifth restoration (head) occurred in 1860 when Francis II renounced himself as emperor and Napoleon became the head of the Roman Empire. However, Napoleon was defeated by the British-led coalition in 1814. This is exactly 1,260 years—554 BCE to AD 1814, forty-two months of thirty days mentioned earlier in Revelation 13:3-5. After Napoleon, Germany and Italy remained divided for some years. However, in 1929, Mussolini signed a treaty with the pope, which ended the bad blood between them that was started in 1870 by Victor

Emmanuel when he had defeated the pope's army. In the meantime, Hitler came to power in Germany in 1933, and he signed a treaty with Rome. This Hitler and Mussolini tie-up was the sixth restoration (head). This head was destroyed in the Second World War. According to the Bible, there is one more restoration, the seventh head, to occur. This seventh head will be defeated at the Armageddon and kept in chains for a thousand years. This head when released for a hundred years will become the eighth head that will take the world into perdition.

This seventh head will consist of ten rulers/leaders/ kings who will be led by one powerful leader who will cheat all nations and lead them into Armageddon. Are we looking at the European Union?

Recession has brought the mighty America down, and the great British Empire is now history. Germany is once again dominating the European scene. History tells us that the Germans have always had a tremendous zeal to rule the world because they believe that theirs is a superior race among all the races of the world. The Bible also tell us that a powerful leader will lead an army from the north (Europe) into the Middle East (Jerusalem), which will lead to Armageddon. Looking at history, we can intelligently guess who this northern king, the leader of the ten nations could be. Ample food for thought!

Stubborn people whose minds have been closed, who do not want to believe even when they see the truth with solid evidence may well say that the above is a cleverly knit story (the Bible and history). Fortunately, there are two more proofs (prophecies) in the Bible that compliment the above truth. These two prophecies were written by two different people in Biblical language and at two different times in history. They are independent of each other and differently described from Nebuchadnezzar's dream we were discussing earlier. But they point out to the same events. After reading these prophecies, it will be impossible not to accept their essence and to argue that they are coincidental.

Chapter VII

Transition—Past to Present: Second Proof

As mentioned earlier, two different people had prophesied the second proof in the way it was given to them. Prophet Daniel wrote the first proof, and John of Revelation wrote the second one many years later. To avoid confusion, let me explain here that Daniel's dream that I am going to narrate now is his own dream and has nothing to do with King Nebuchadnezzar's dream or his son Belshazzar's dream that he had interpreted and we had discussed earlier. Daniel, in his old age, sees a series of visions. These are mentioned in Daniel 7, 8, 9, 10, 11, and 12. Unfortunately, I am unable to reproduce them all here because of the length of the passages, except the vision in Daniel 7 after three paragraphs because it has direct connection with King Nebuchadnezzar's dream with the huge statue and John's vision of the beast. But I earnestly request the reader to take time and read the rest of them without fail for concrete proof, clear and absolute understanding.

A very important point to note here is that when Daniel wrote his visions, he was writing entirely about the future (none of the events of his vision had taken place). That is why God tells him in Daniel 12:4 that, "And now, Daniel, close the book and put a seal on it until the end of the world." Then in verse 9, God says, "You must go now, Daniel, because these words are to be kept secret and hidden until the end time comes."

The second proof (vision) was written by John, Jesus' youngest apostle, whom Jesus loved more than any other, six hundred years after Daniel, in the first century AD.

Unlike Daniel, John sees only one beast with seven heads yet with all the characteristics of the four beasts of Daniel's prophecy. This is because the three beasts of Daniel had passed into history. Therefore, John was shown only one beast with seven heads and ten horns—the ten end-time figures/kings. The point to note here is that while Daniel received his visions from God, John's vision was given to him by Jesus as his apostle, not as a doomsday warning as falsely preached by some quarters but as powerful and true encouragement for people about Jesus' second coming as King of Kings and Lord of Lords, and so to remain faithful to God in spite of all the interim tragic events.

Daniel's Vision (Daniel 7)

To make things easier for the reader, I will insert the interpretation of the intellectuals along with the vision. In his vision, Daniel saw four beasts come out of the ocean, a lion with wings like an eagle. Its wings were torn off, and it was made to stand as a man, and a human mind was given it. This parallels with the Babylonian Empire, the head of gold of Nebuchadnezzar's statue. The second beast was like a bear standing on its hind legs. It was holding three ribs between its teeth, and a voice said to it, "Go on, and eat as much as you can." The voice and three ribs indicate that the beast would be ferocious and devour every one. This would be the ferocious Medo-Persian Empire, the chest of silver and two hands of Nebuchadnezzar's statue. The third beast was like a leopard, but on its back, there were four wings, and it had four heads. It had a look of authority about it. This would be Alexander's Hellenistic Empire. The four wings would mean that he would fly to the end of the world to conquer it, and the four heads would be his four generals who would became kings after his death. This would be the waist and hips of bronze of Nebuchadnezzar's statue. The fourth beast was unlike the other three (incomparable to the other three beasts). It was very powerful and had iron teeth with which it crushed all its victims. This would be the divided Roman Empire from 31 BCE to AD 1945, consisting of various kings and leaders ruling at various times during its seven restorations—the two long legs of iron of the statue. The ten horns on the fourth beast would be the ten kings/leaders who, with the final single ruler, would lead the world into Armageddon. The little horn that tore the three horns would be the bishop of Rome who had helped to overthrow the Vandals, the Heruli, and the Ostrogoths that led the way to Imperial Restoration in AD 554.

Now, as mentioned earlier, John wrote his vision about six hundred years after Daniel and about seventy to eighty years after Jesus' death, resurrection, and ascension to heaven. At that time, Christianity had spread far and wide in the Middle Eastern region. Seeing this, the Romans began unprecedented persecution of the Christians in Jerusalem. Therefore, many Christians had fled from the city. John was among those who had fled and was at the island of Patmos in the Mediterranean Sea. At that time, Jesus gave this vision to John and asked him to record it so that Christians will know what will happen in the future and be prepared for it by remaining faithful to their faith, which they had newly acquired. Jesus wanted his followers to know that though the immediate future looked bleak and full of turmoil, he will come back soon and set things right for all eternity. By soon he meant that when all the prophecies will be fulfilled, but the Christians thought that he would come during their lifetime. We have to remember that John's beast was the fourth beast of Daniel seen in a different way.

Now let us look into John's vision in Revelation 13. He sees a beast coming out of the sea. It had seven heads and ten horns. Unlike Daniel, John sees only one beast because, as mentioned earlier, the three beasts of Daniel had already passed into history. The seven heads of John's beast represented the seven revivals of the Roman Empire. The ten horns with crowns represented the ten end-time kings/leaders who would join the (lone) powerful leader (Satan's representative) who would lead the world into perdition. The powerful leader is introduced to us in Revelation 13:11-17 as another beast. This beast speaks like a dragon because the dragon, the great serpent of old, called the Devil and Satan (Revelation

12:9) had given the Beast (the lone leader) its own power, his throne, and his authority (Revelation 13:2b). Then Revelation 12 and onwards says that, the lone leader will use its vast authority given by the first beast, Satan, to force the people of the earth to worship the first beast. To do this, it will perform great miracles and deceive all the people of the earth. "The whole earth was amazed and followed the beast. Every one followed the dragon because he had given authority to the beast. They worshipped the beast also saying, who is like the beast, who can fight against it?" In John's vision, the second beast (the lone leader) had two horns like the lamb's horns. Those would be two superpowers of the world of the end time that the lone leader will deceive and control and take into perdition.

I believe that the events that have taken place so far in history when seen in the light of the Bible prophecies give enough proof that after God created the world, he did not get fed up with the sins of humans and their disobedience and let it tend for itself as some believe and preach. But God was and is actively involved in human affairs. In the beginning, he gave us patriarchs to lead us, then he gave us kings. When the kings began to lead the people into evil ways, he sent the prophets to warn and guide us. When this failed, he sent his only begotten Son Jesus to draw us to himself. Looking at the current situation, it appears that even Jesus has failed. But we have to remember that God did not send Jesus to save the whole world. He sent Jesus to remind us about the forgotten ways of God, the Ten Commandments. Jesus would accomplish this task by living and teaching God's ways. Jesus' task was to reconcile us to himself first and then to God by destroying the power of sin and thus the power of evil, once and for all. And this task, Jesus would accomplish by virtue of his agonizing passion and death on the cross. God sent Jesus only to obtain salvation for us and to show us the way of salvation so that we can save ourselves collectively through our efforts and his grace. It is very plain and obvious that if God wanted to save the world through Jesus, he would have allowed Jesus to wield his godly power to do so. God would not have allowed Jesus to lead the life of an ordinary prophet, preaching and performing a few miracles and then die a miserable death thereby causing misunderstanding among people that God and Jesus have both failed. The mere fact that

Jesus chose twelve apostles and gathered many disciples clearly indicates that he would train them thoroughly, obtain reconciliation and friendship with God through his death, and then instruct them to go into the whole world (Mark 16:15-18) and teach the way of salvation. The above passage clearly tells us that it was God's plan that human beings should learn from Jesus and realize their mistakes (sins) and obtain their own salvation by following Jesus' lifestyle. That is why God inspired the New Testament to be written—so that future generations will know exactly what happened and follow the Bible to obtain their salvation. However, realization of our mistakes and conviction of our sins would come through Jesus' Holy Spirit because Jesus would not be seen physically alive on earth till he comes again at the end time, except for a short period after his resurrection. Therefore, forty days after Jesus' ascension on Pentecost Day, Jesus sent his Holy Spirit on the Apostles in the form of tongues of fire (Acts 2:1-12). Christians receive this Holy Spirit at baptism. In Matthew 28:19-20, Jesus solemnly orders the disciples to "go, then, to all peoples everywhere and make them my disciples; baptize them in the name of the Father, of the Son, and of the Holy Spirit, and teach them to obey everything I have commanded you. And I will be with you always, to the end of the age." The Holy Spirit guides the life of people as long as people live reasonably good lives.

If the seed of possibility that the Bible is the true word of God has been sown in the hearts and minds of my readers, then it would be quite easy for you to understand what is written in the rest of this book. So let us go to the next chapter.

Chapter VIII

Present to End Time

Now we have come to the final chapter, a chapter in which we will deal with the prophesied end time, Jesus' second coming, the raising of the dead, the three judgments, the New Heaven and the New Earth, and God's eternal kingdom. Basically, we will deal with the book of Revelation.

But first, we need to recognize that though the events in the book of Revelation will and are meant to occur in sequence, they seem to have been written haphazardly and repeated in different places, creating confusion. This confusion has and is causing difficulty to a casual reader to understand, believe, and accept the truth mentioned therein. Besides, there are certain terms used that need to be understood not only in their text and context but also in their connection to the entire narrative of the Bible and especially their specific intended purposes. Therefore, a word of caution seems necessary here. That is, my readers would need a lot of patience to go through this part of the book. However, I would like to impress upon and encourage you that in the light of the information you have gathered so far in this book, it would be quite easy for you to follow and understand. Unfortunately, I too will have to repeat certain events every now and then. But since I will be arranging them in an explanatory order to the best of my ability, I believe it will be easy for you to understand. I may also have to go off the track sometimes to show the connection. But I can assure you that the outcome of your patience will be rewarding and very beneficial. Having come thus far, it is imperative that you continue to read and understand the truth about the whole purpose of human existence.

A. The Prophesied End Time

During the time of the prophets (during the reign of the kings of the divided Israelite kingdom), people came to believe that the duration of the world order would be seven thousand years. This belief originated during the time of Prophet Elijah. This was drawn from God's six days of creation work and one day of Sabbath rest program (Exodus 20:8-11) and King David's Psalm 90:4, "A thousand years to you are like one day." St. Peter confirmed this period of one day equals to one thousand years many centuries later in his letter to the Christians. He wrote, "But do not forget one thing my dear friends; there is no difference in the Lord's sight between one day and a 1000 years; to him the two are the same" (2 Peter 3:8). Thus, each day of creation was accepted as a thousand years. Human beings would govern the first six thousand years. This is because God had initially planned to govern the people, but Adam's sin upset his plan, and so he decided to govern them through his directly appointed representatives (like Abraham). But by the time Elijah came on the scene, the Israelites had demanded a king (as the pagans did) to rule them (1 Samuel 8:4-5). Though God was much displeased, his great mercy would allow this to happen for a specific end time reason (explained later).

Mostly, corrupt kings ruled the divided kingdom, and the trend still continues though the kingdoms have become countries governed by corrupt leaders. This will continue till the six thousand years are over. At the end of the six thousandth year, God will send Emmanuel, which means "God with us," Jesus, his Son, to rule this world physically. All the people living at that time will be taught God's ways (different from nearly six thousand years of corrupt ways) by Jesus and his chosen group of people.

Many scholars and theologians believe that we are at the last quarter of the last minute of the six thousand-year period (this is also mentioned in the reproduced e-mail). It is quite easy to accept this belief by a careful study of the Bible. If we add the ages of each patriarch to Noah's age after the flood, we get a figure of 1,556 years (Genesis 5:3-29). Then Genesis 11:10-32 indicates that, 427 years had passed from the time of the flood to the death of Terah (Abraham's father) when Abraham left Haran. Abraham was seventy-five years old then. When Abraham was a hundred years old, Isaac was born (Genesis 21:5), which means fifty-two years after Abraham left Haran. From Isaac's birth to Exodus (coming out of Egypt) it was 430 years (Genesis 15:13). Four hundred eighty years had passed from Exodus to beginning of construction of the first original temple by King Solomon (1 Kings 6:1). History tells us that approximately 966 years had passed after the construction of the first temple when Jesus Christ was born in Bethlehem. If we add these figures of 1556+427+430+480+966, we will get a figure of 3,859 years. We are in the year 2010, which makes it 5,869 years, which is close to the end of 6,000 years. This means that we are also close to Jesus' second coming—close to Armageddon (Third World War) and closer to the prophesied end time, 6000-5869=131. Looking at this figure, the current generation, both the old as well as the young, may be tempted to relax with the thought that nothing will happen in these 131 years, but we have to remember that the Bible warns us of unprecedented suffering before the final catastrophe. A careful observer will notice that we are experiencing many of the minor ones already. I am calling the current suffering minor in comparison with the suffering mentioned in Revelation 16: 15, 16, and 17 that are going to befall on all humans. Please read these passages.

The battle of Armageddon will not be like any of the previous wars were man fought against man for selfish reasons, material gain, hatred, domination, etc. This war will be fought for the destruction of the evil and establishment of justice and peace and equality for all. This war will be similar in dimension to the catastrophic war fought between the good angels and the bad angels that I had mentioned in an earlier chapter.

It is absolutely important to understand here that end time does not mean the "end of the world," not at all. It simply means two-thirds of the world and its inhabitants will be destroyed. The one-third who will survive will enter the Millennium Rule of Christ (mentioned in the e-mail) to construct a new uncorrupt world order (explained later). Readers are requested to read Matthew 24:2-12 and 29-31, Luke 21:25-28, and Joel 2:30-32 and pay close attention to the passages mentioned therein. Thus, the prophesied end time means end of six thousand years of the corrupt world order.

Before we discuss the second coming of Jesus, we should be familiar with the words death and Hades and the subtitles following them.

Death

Death as we all know is an undeniable fact of life, which comes sooner or later to every one. It is universally accepted that in death, the body is separated from the soul/breath/spirit. The body is wasted away, but the soul/breath/spirit, which is supposed to be immortal, remains for all eternity. But is this absolutely true? The answer is yes and no. Let me explain. God is the creator of everything; therefore, he has the power and control over all things. He put the breath into human beings. Naturally therefore, he holds absolute power and authority either to sustain it or destroy it. He has clearly warned us through Prophet Ezekiel 18:4—"Behold all souls are mine; the soul of the father as well as the soul of the son is mine, the soul who sins shall die." So the soul can die or be destroyed or, as the Bible says, burnt up (Revelation 20:13-15). This burning up will surely take place only once and only after the third and final judgment. Until then, there will be three resurrections of the bodies, and the separated souls of those bodies will be given back to them (explained later). Thus, the worldly death is only temporary. There will be a permanent death of Satan, his demons, and the rejected souls at the White Throne (final) Judgment.

Hades

Hades has been misunderstood through misinterpretation as hell, a place of eternal fire where Satan reigns and his demons torture the souls of the wicked forever. My belief is that the earlier authorities of all religions manufactured this misinterpretation to keep the followers under control.

This is both good and bad. Good because fear of eternal damnation did cause majority of the people to think twice before embarking on a wrong deed. It was definitely a positive incentive against a negative action. Bad because through the induction of too much fear, human beings were made slaves and taken advantage of.

Truthfully, Hades simply means the "world of the dead," where souls of the dead rest till their resurrection. This is where Jesus rested for three days before his resurrection. This is what the Catholics proclaim every time they recite the Apostle's Creed (He was crucified, died and was buried. He descended to the dead). This is where Lazarus rested for four days before Jesus raised him up (John 11:38-44). Therefore, this is where all the souls—the good, the bad, and the ugly—will rest until they are raised in God's proper time. So what is hell? We will take a tour of it later in the chapter.

B. The Period of Tribulation

The period of tribulation mentioned in the Bible is a period of unprecedented trouble of three and a half years for all humanity. This will occur just after Jesus' coming in the air (not on earth). Please note that Jesus' second coming is in two phases. The first coming is only in the air and the second coming is on earth, not as a child this time but as a fully grown person (explained later). The period of tribulation will occur between the coming in the air and coming on the earth. The four horses, the sixth seal, and the seven angels with trumpets symbolically yet truly describe what will happen during those three and a half years. I would suggest my readers to read about this in the book of Revelation but only after you have read and understood the simplified explanation provided by me. This period of tribulation is also mentioned symbolically in the book of Isaiah 13:6-13—"Howl in pain! The day of the Lord is near, the day when the Almighty brings destruction. Every one's hands will hang limp, and every one's courage will fail. They will be terrified and overcome with pain, like the pain of a woman in labor. They will look at each other in fear, and their faces will burn in shame. The day of the Lord is coming—that cruel day of his fierce anger and fury. The earth will be made a wilderness, and every sinner will be destroyed. Every star every constellation will stop shining, the sun will be dark when it rises, and the moon will give no light" (also mentioned in the e-mail).

The Lord says, "I will bring disaster on the earth and punish all wicked people for their sins. I will humble every one who is proud and punish every one who is arrogant and cruel. Those who survive will be scarcer than gold. I will make the heaven tremble, the earth will be shaken out of its place on that day when I, the Lord Almighty, show my anger" (also mentioned in the e-mail). Also read the book of Prophet Joel 2:1-11 and Luke 23:30. This tribulation will affect all people but will be especially targeted toward the Jews. God himself will allow this to happen to the Jews because through this suffering, he would provide them an opportunity to awaken from their slumber caused by the devil, change their way of life, and follow a life according to his teachings before Jesus comes to hold a special judgment just before his Millennium Rule on earth. Only those who prove to be faithful will enter the Millennium Rule (Zechariah 14:5, also read 13:7-9). This period is also called as the time of Jacob's trouble in some versions of the Bible (Jeremiah 30:7). When we say, "Jews," it does not mean Jews living only in the area of Jerusalem, but it means Jews, the descendents of Jacob, spread all over the entire world under various nationalities. This clearly indicates that the tribulation will not be only in Jerusalem and its surroundings but will spread to all nations and all people.

C. The Daily

Daily simply means daily sacrifice. It is also known as the continual in the Bible. However, this simple-sounding sacrifice has a great significance to our future because this sacrifice is God's continuous work on earth by the church established by Jesus. This sacrifice should and will continue till Jesus' second coming on earth. However, this daily will be suspended twice, first during the time of tribulation (explained later). This suspension will be brought about deceitfully and yet forcefully by the Antichrist and will last for 1,150 days. It will be caused by the transgression of the Antichrist who will appear at that time (Daniel 8:11-14).

Jesus will cause the second time suspension when he comes to earth. This time, the daily will be suspended because those who purify and convert themselves during the tribulation—the elite—will be taken to a safe place (secret destination) by Jesus, and he will ask them to suspend the daily while they are there to safeguard them from the Antichrist. This is what Jesus meant to his Apostles when he said, "Two men will be working in a field, one will be taken away, and the other will be left behind. Two women will be at a mill, grinding meal, one will be taken away, and the other will be left behind" (Matthew 24:40-41). This suspension will last only for a few days because the battle of Armageddon will commence and the Antichrist and his false prophets will be destroyed and Satan will be chained and locked for a thousand years.

Who is this anti-Christ, or how do we identify him when he appears on the world scene? How would people recognize him hundred percent after so many false identifications over the years! Fortunately, the inspired book, the Bible, interprets and explains itself but only to those who have the patience to look for clues.

In the year 176 BCE, Antiochus Epiphanes was king of Syria of the fast-declining Greco-Macedonian Empire. History tells us that he took control of the country as king through deceit, lies, and pretension of compliance to the Roman authority initially. But within a few years, he took complete control and claimed himself to be god. History also tells us that he brought unprecedented terror during his reign. Daniel 11:21-45 corroborates with what history tells us. Why is he important to our discussion? The answer to this is having claimed to be god, he banned the daily sacrifice of the Jews and set up an awful horror in the temple of the Jews (Daniel 11:29-31) and forced everyone to worship this awful horror. Daniel had prophesied this Antiochus in 548 BCE during the reign of Cyrus the Great, 372 years earlier. Daniel, in his vision in chapter 11:8-3, tells us that he saw a ram with two horns, one longer than the other. In verse 20, we are told that, these two horns are the kings of Media and Persia (historical evidence). In verse 5 of chapter 8, we are told that he sees a goat rushing out of the west that had a prominent horn between its eyes. Verse 21 explains that the goat represents the king of Greece, and the prominent horn between the eyes is the first king. History tells us that the first king is Alexander the Great. In verse 8 of chapter 8, we are told that the goat vexed very greatly, and when he was strong and prominent, his horn was broken, and in its place, four notable horns came up. History tells us that Alexander died at the zenith of his power and four of his generals divided the kingdom into four parts and ruled. Daniel 8 verse 9 continues, "And out of the four horns came forth a little horn, which vexed exceedingly great." Most of the religious and historical commentators agree that this little horn is Antiochus Epiphanes. We have to remember that Daniel's prophecy was meant not only for the near future but for the prophesied end time also. Daniel 12:4 reads, "He said to me, 'And now, Daniel, close the book and put a seal on it until the end of the world.'"

Therefore, since Daniel's prophecies have all come true, word for word in the past, it is accepted in the Christian circle that another ruler/leader of the type of Antiochus will appear on the world scene toward the end time, and he too will do exactly the same as Antiochus did. Especially, he will force the churches to stop the daily sacrifice (God's work). He will establish his own religion (nonreligion) and claim himself to be god and will be the cause of the terrible tribulation we have been discussing. Millions will succumb to his terror tactics and abandon God.

If we even remotely believe that we are in the last quarter of the last minute of the six thousand years, then we can expect the end-time Antiochus to appear soon enough. It would be wise to keep our hearts clean, minds and eyes open and look around and recognize the visible signs around us, especially the developments in Europe. We have to understand here that the 5,869 years mentioned earlier should be taken as a tentative figure as it is widely believed that we are actually much closer to the end of 6,000th year, the end of end time.

D. Abomination of Desolation

This will occur during the time period of the tribulation and is directly connected to it. According to the Bible, the Antichrist will be the abomination, the loathsome and corrupt tyrant. Like Antiochus of ancient, he will make a firm treaty with the neighboring countries for seven years of peace and friendship. But within three and a half years, he will gain full control over the entire world and create havoc among all people for the remaining three and a half years. He will ban the daily sacrifice, and because of which, the churches will remain desolate for some time.

Like the suspension of the daily, this desolation will be caused because of the transgression of the Antichrist. Similarly, there will be another desolation of a few days just before Armageddon because of the suspension of the daily by Jesus. This, as mentioned earlier, will be to safeguard the righteous people. This incident is also mentioned in the book of Revelation chapter 12. Thus, we can clearly see the connection (continuation) between the vision of Daniel and John, a sort of sequel to verse 12 of Daniel and Revelation 12 although there is a time difference of many centuries.

In Revelation 12, John sees a woman (symbol of a church in the Bible) whose dress was the sun and who had the moon under her feet and a crown of twelve stars on her head (sign of glory and universality of the church). This woman is crying out with pain and suffering of childbirth (tribulation). Then John sees a great dragon (the Antichrist) with seven heads and ten horns (fourth beast of Daniel 7). This dragon wants to devour the child, but the child is taken to God, and the woman flees to the desert (symbol of safety) to a place God had prepared for her, where she will be taken care of for 1,260 days. This simply means that toward the end of the tribulation, when everything looks hopeless for all humans, Jesus will arrive suddenly (childbirth). But the dragon Antichrist will try to destroy Jesus and his followers. But God will protect Jesus, and Jesus will protect the church. While the Antichrist will cause the desolation to destroy goodness from earth, Jesus will cause a temporary desolation to safeguard the church from total destruction toward the approach of Armageddon.

E. The Antichrist and the Number 666

We have referred to the Antichrist quite a few times in the last chapter. Therefore, it is necessary to know how to identify this Antichrist. Although no specific name is mentioned, the Bible provides enough clues to watch for when he appears.

First Clue

In Revelation 13:18, we come across the mysterious number 666. The passage reads, "This calls for wisdom, whoever is intelligent can figure out the meaning of the number of the beast because the number stands for a man's name. Its number is 666."

The previous chapter, 16:17, says, "The beast forced 'all' the people small and great, rich and poor, slave and free, to have a mark to be placed on their right hand or their forehead. No one could buy or sell [complete control], unless he had this mark; that is the beast's name or the number that stands for the name." These two passages clearly explain that this number 666 is the identity of a man, and this man will gain authority over every tribe, nation, language, and race—in one word, all people (literally). The entire chapter 13 of the book of Revelation tells us about this man and his activities.

To understand this number 666, we have to remember that the book of Revelation was written in Greek. The Greek writers referred to the Roman Empire by the term Latinos. We know that Greek alphabets have numbers, so Latinos adds up to 666. L=30; a=1; t=300; e=5; i=10; n=50; o=70; s=200. Therefore, the owner of this number 666 will be the man (ruler/leader) of the revived (for the seventh and the last time) vast Roman Empire. We have already discussed the seventh revival earlier.

Second Clue

The Antichrist is also likened to Emperor Nero of Rome. He too came to power by deceitful promises of a golden age but turned into a ruthless tyrant. He ordered the persecution and possible annihilation of Christians. His full name was Nero Caesar, which in Greek is Neron Kaesar. When this name is spelt in Hebrew, the numerical value adds up to 666. Nero is likened to Antiochus Epiphanes and Nimrod, the first postflood tyrant

(Genesis 10:8). If we remember, Nimrod had also started off as a good king but later proclaimed to be a god and led the people to abandon the creator God and follow his own religion.

Third Clue

History tells us that the nation of Rome got its name from its founder Romulus. In Latin, it is written as "Romvls" whose numerical value adds up to 666. This again indicates the connection between the Antichrist and the Roman Empire. What the passage 18 of Revelations 13 simply means is that the Roman Empire will be resurrected one final time by two beasts of Revelation 13. The first beast will be Satan himself, and he will raise a man to be his counterfeit and give all his authority and even miraculous powers to this man. As God the Father will send Jesus into this world to establish his goodness in the world, so also Satan will raise an Antichrist at the end time to destroy goodness from earth (remember Satan has retained all his initial powers because God does not take what he once gives). These two combined will lead the world into unimaginable chaos and suffering and into Armageddon. If we carefully observe and follow the current happenings in the world in the light of all these biblical facts mentioned in this book, it will be very easy to get the hint that the Antichrist will surely rise from Europe, especially from the vicinity of Rome, and Armageddon and Jesus' second coming is just around the next corner.

F. Time, Times, and Half a Time

In some versions of the Bible in the book of Revelation 12:14, we come across another term—time, times, and half a time. Until I learnt the meaning, this term used to confuse me. Therefore, I believe it is good for the readers to know what it means. It simply means "three and a half years." Time=one year; times=twice one year=two years; half a time=half of one year=half year. This relates directly to the three and a half years of tribulation we had discussed earlier. But how do we know that the meaning is true? Do we have any connection in the Bible to corroborate it? For this, we have to go back to the Old Testament once again. In the book of Daniel chapter 4, we read that Nebuchadnezzar, king of Babylon, in his second dream was told that he would be punished for his pride and vanity. His punishment would be that he would lose his sanity and banished from his kingdom for seven years and live in the jungle with wild animals eating grass. History tells us that he did lose his sanity and fled to the forest and literally lived like an animal for seven years. Then when he repented, he was restored back to his kingdom. Please read this fascinating fact of history in Daniel 4:10-37.

In an earlier chapter, we have already discussed the "seven-time punishment" (delay) of 2,520 years. Thus, seven times in this context is seven literal years, which is 2,520 days, 84 months of 30 days. Half of 2,520 days is 1,260 days, which is three and a half years, which is time, times, and a half time. This is significant because this is the time between Jesus' coming in the air (first resurrection of the dead) and Jesus' coming on the earth (just before Armageddon). These will be the seven years during which time the Antichrist will rule the world. Out of these seven years, the world will suffer tribulation for three and a half years.

G. Jesus's Second Coming

For better understanding, Jesus' second coming should be considered in two phases.

The First Phase

The first phase is known as the Rupture of the Church, which means "to catch away." This will be the first of a series of events that will occur during the end time. During this period, Jesus will appear in the air with a sudden loud sound of the trumpet, and in the blink of an eye, all the dead Christians from the time of Jesus will rise with their original soul and bodies and meet up with Jesus in the air. Simultaneously, all the righteous living on earth will also be taken to Jesus in the air. This event is described by St. Paul in 1 Thessalonians 4:16-17: "The Lord himself will descend from heaven with a shout with the voice of an Archangel, and with the trumpet of God, and the dead in 'Christ' will rise first. Then the living that believe in Christ, shall be caught up together with them in the clouds to meet the Lord in the air. Then Christ will take them to be with himself always." In the Gospel of John, we read Jesus telling his Apostles just before he went to the Garden of Gethsemane where he was arrested, "Do not be worried or upset, believe in God and believe also in me. There are many rooms in my Father's house, and I am going to prepare a place for you. I would not tell you this if it were not so. And after I go and prepare a place for you, I will come back and take you to myself. So that you will be where I am." (Read Isaiah 26:19.) The remaining dead from the time of Adam will continue to rest till the final judgment (explained later).

I believe that "take them to be with him always" mentioned above needs some explanation. We have to remember here that Jesus will first come in the air and raise the dead Christians, gather them, and also gather the living righteous on earth to himself in the air. Then he will hold the first judgment (explained later), assign them their task on earth, and will go back. However, he will not physically "take them to be with him" because he will need them to do his work on earth. So he will keep them on earth and fill them with his grace to live in his spirit and remain faithful to him. Living in his grace will actually be like living in his presence and in union with him. Also, he will not need to take them away anywhere because he will be coming back to earth just before Armageddon and will be living here on earth. Thus, he will be taking them to be with him always here on earth forever anyway. "There are many rooms . . . so that you will be where I am" mentioned above also means the same thing.

However, among those taken to Jesus in the air, 144,000 (Revelation 7:1-8) will be specially chosen by Jesus and will be given immortality. They will be appointed as his kings/rulers, priests, and administrators, etc., in his Millennium Kingdom.

There is a teaching going around in some Christian circle that among all the billions of people God created, he will only save the 144,000, and the rest are doomed to perish in hell. This is a gross misinterpretation of this text. This misinterpretation must have been picked up from

Revelation 14:3—"The 144,000 people stood before the throne, the four living creatures, and the elders; they were singing a new song, which only they could learn. Of all the mankind they are the only ones who have been redeemed." My interpretation and understanding of the phrase "only ones who have been redeemed" is that it does not mean that God will save only those 144,000 people, but what it does mean is that they are the only ones who will be redeemed from mortality and given immortality at Jesus's coming in the air. It is unimaginable for any one to believe that a merciful God who created humans out of pure love and who loves humans unconditionally all the time should grant eternity to only 144,000 people and let the other billions to perish. This teaching is in stark contradiction to God's words in Isaiah 49:15—"Can a woman forget her own baby and not love the child she bore? Even if a mother should forget her child, I will never forget you." Of course God who is a father to all will punish those who deserve punishment but only after giving every one repeated opportunities to make themselves worthy of eternal reward. So who are these 144,000 John was talking about? We get a clear clue in Revelation 20:4-6: "Then I saw thrones, and those who sat on them were given the power to judge, I also saw the souls of those who had been executed because they had not worshipped the beast or its image, nor had they received the mark of the beast on their forehead or their hand. They came to life and ruled as kings with Christ for a thousand years." Then verse 6 says, "Greatly blessed are those who are included in the first raising of the dead. The second death has no power over them [immortality]. They shall be princes of God and of Christ and they will rule with him for a thousand years."

The 144,000 will not be God's favorites but those who had earned their place to be the one among those specially chosen. They will be the martyrs and those executed for the faith. Those who had silently endured persecution for the faith, the extraordinary faithful people who had followed God's commands and Jesus' teaching in an extraordinary way and who had rendered extraordinary service in the world, like the saints for example. As mentioned earlier, they will be given high positions in Jesus' kingdom. In Revelation 22:12, Jesus tells John, "'Listen,' says Jesus, 'I am coming soon,

I will bring my reward with me to give to each one according to what he had done. I am the first and the last, the beginning and the end.'"

The remaining people taken to Jesus in the air will stand in judgment before Christ. This judgment is called the Judgment Seat of Christ. The issue at this judgment will not be condemnation, punishment, or salvation. Condemnation and salvation will come for all (except the 144,000) at the last White Throne Judgment. The issue at this judgment will be who will receive what reward (position) in Jesus' Millennium Rule. The reward will be according to his/her faithfulness to him during their lifetime on earth. St. Paul in 2 Corinthians 5:10 tells us, "We must all appear before the judgment seat of Christ, that each one may receive the things done in the body, according to what he had done, whether good or bad." The three parables of Jesus in Luke 19:17-27, Matthew 20:1-6, and 25:14-30 clearly point toward this event. The judgment will determine the role they will play and the position they will hold in Jesus' Millennium Rule. Read also Revelation 4:10 and 5:8.

After the judgment is over, the 144,000 and the rest will be sent back to earth once again. Having seen Jesus face-to-face, most of them will remain faithful to him forever. Although John has named only the Twelve Tribes of Israel specifically in Revelation 7:5-8, we have to remember that these Twelve Tribes have spread all over the world into various nations. Thus the 144,000 will be chosen from among all the nations and will be placed all over the world to look after the administration of the entire world. There is ample indication that apart from the 144,000, the other faithful sent down to earth will rule too. In Luke 19:11-19, in the parable of the gold coins, we read, "'Well done,' he said, 'you are a good servant; since you were faithful in very little, have authority over ten cities.'" St. Paul in 1 Corinthians 6:2-3 says, "Don't you know that God's people will judge [rule] the world?"

The Second Phase

As the activities of the first phase are taking place, the Antichrist would come on the world scene and would begin to gather his followers first with deceit and exhibition of even magical powers and later by force. Unfortunately, some of the people who had experienced Jesus in the air would be deceived and follow the Antichrist with the unrighteous left behind during Jesus' coming in the air. Unable to tolerate the good works being done by God's people, the Antichrist will start a terrible persecution (tribulation) of the righteous people. He will ban the daily and will set up the abomination and create the desolation of the church during the second half of his seven years' reign (for three and a half years). During these three and a half years, he will gather a huge bloodthirsty army consisting of people who would resist God's teaching during the tribulation. They will be trained to hate and try to annihilate God's faithful people. This army will march toward Megiddo (Revelation 16:12-16). Meanwhile having realized the deceitful and selfish intention of the anti Christ, the northern and the eastern kingdoms will form their own armies and fight against the Antichrist. This battle will take place in Jerusalem, and God's faithful people, especially the Jews, will face unimaginable pain and suffering (Jacob's trouble). But they will be kept safe (the second suspension of the daily). Millions will die during this period not only because of this war but also because of other natural calamities; read Zechariah 14:12 and 15.

Who are the kings of the north and the east? If we check the world map, we see that Europe is to the north of Jerusalem (not directly and not very close though). Europe has formed a union in which Germany is the dominating power. Germany has the history of two world wars. Could this union be the seventh and the last revival of the Roman Empire? India and China though far are directly to the east of Jerusalem. In the past few years, these two countries have been gaining tremendous economical power and technological know-how and are on the verge of becoming superpowers. Could they combine and become the army of the east? Possibilities are very strong because in Revelation 9:16, we read, "The four Angels were released; for the very hour of this day of this very month and year, they had been kept ready to kill a third of all mankind. I was told the number of the mounted troops; it was 200 million." Which nations other than India and China combined would be able to raise such a large army?

When everything seems hopeless and annihilation eminent, at the end of the Antichrist's seven years rule, Jesus will physically descend on the Mount of Olives, not as a child this time but exactly as he ascended to heaven in the presence of his Apostles. In the book of Acts, we read of the encouragement those Apostles received. "After saying this, He was taken up to heaven as they watched him, and a cloud hid him from their sight. They still had their eyes fixed on the sky as he went away, when two men dressed in white suddenly stood beside them and said, 'Galileans, why are you standing there looking at the sky? This Jesus, who was taken from you into heaven, will come back in the same way that you saw him go to heaven'" (Acts 1: 9-11). Prophet Zechariah had prophesied many centuries before Jesus was born, between 520-518 BCE—"At that time He will stand on the Mount of Olives, to the east of Jerusalem. Then the Mount of Olives will split in two from east to west by a large valley. Half of the mountain will move northward and half of it southward" (Zechariah 14: 4).

John has described the second phase very beautifully in Revelation 19:11-13: "Then I saw heaven open, and there was a white horse. Its rider is called Faithful and True; it is with justice that he judges and fights his battles. His eyes were like flame of fire, and he wore many crowns on his head. He had a name written on him, but no one except himself knows what it is. The robe he wore was covered with blood. His name is the Word of God." As soon as Jesus sets his feet on the Mount of Olives, all his followers will be gathered into an army. The Antichrist who had already marched into Jerusalem will prepare for battle with Jesus. A strange and unusual event will take place at that time. God will cause the king of the north and the king of the east to join the Antichrist (though they had initially come to fight against him). This battle will be the fiercest battle that was ever fought by humans, the famous Armageddon, the Third World War. Good news is that Jesus will crush his enemies. The Antichrist and his false Prophets will be killed, as well as millions of his followers. Then Satan will be locked in the abyss (not hell) for a thousand years. Revelation 20:1-3 clearly states this: "Then I saw an Angel coming down from heaven, holding in his hand the key of the abyss [not hell] and a heavy chain, he seized the dragon, that ancient serpent, that is the devil or Satan, and chained him up for a thousand years. The Angel threw him into the abyss [not hell], locked it and sealed it, so that he could not deceive the nations any more until the 1000 years were over." However, Satan will be let loose for a little while after the thousand years are over (explained later).

Why would Satan be locked up for a thousand years? The answer is during these thousand years, Jesus will rule as king over all the earth. He is holy and pure; therefore, during his reign, nothing evil can and will exist. Prophet Isaiah wrote, "On Zion, God's holy hill, there will be nothing harmful or evil; the land will be full of knowledge of the Lord as the seas are full of water" (Isaiah 11:9).

The second reason is we have already discussed that the world order is set for seven thousand years, six thousand for human government, and a thousand years for God's government. The Bible and history tells us that during the past six thousand years, man has devised many systems of government, and all of them up to now have failed miserably. This is because none of them were and are based on God's commandments. Because of man's disobedience and arrogance, God has allowed this to happen and will allow this to continue till the end of the six thousand years. Although God's Word was and is being taught in the world continuously during this time, he has allowed spiritual blindness (promoted by Satan and his ambassadors) to exist in the world. There is a special reason for this, and that is God intends people of all ages to learn a serious and valuable lesson from their mistakes. He wants them to understand and realize the difference between their corrupt government of six thousand years and Jesus' one thousand years of rule with peace, justice, and equality. St. Paul in Romans 11:25-27 tells us, "For I do not desire, brothers, that you should be ignorant of this mystery, lest you should be wise in your own opinion [arrogance], that blindness in part has happened to Israel [all descendents] until the fullness of the Gentiles has come in, and so all Israel will be saved." As scripture says, "The Savior will come from Zion and remove all wickedness from the descendents of Jacob. I will make this covenant with them when I take away their sins." Read also Isaiah 59:20-21. God's intention is that during the thousand years, all the living should realize the difference and turn to him so that when Satan is let loose for a little while after Jesus' rule, they will not be deceived again and follow Satan. Thus, the second phase of Jesus' coming will be to establish his kingdom on earth for a thousand years.

Before going further, it is important to understand that there will be three resurrections and three judgments before God's kingdom is established on earth (not Jesus's Millennium Rule). Some may be surprised to read this, some may even laugh, and some may think that I am talking about reincarnation (Hindus believe in seven of them). Here I am not talking about reincarnation but about the resurrection mentioned in the Bible—like Jesus' resurrection three days after his death (Matthew 28:1-10; Mark 6:1-8; Luke 24:1-12 and John 20:1-10) and Lazarus's resurrection four days after his death [(John 11:38-46). God caused the resurrection of Lazarus as a prelude for our understanding of the resurrections that would occur to humans at the end time. Jesus will conduct these three resurrections (as in the case of Lazarus). The resurrected will have their original soul and body albeit any disease and ailments that troubled them in their previous lives. Read Ezekiel 37:1-14.

First Resurrection

We have already discussed that this will take place when Jesus comes in the air. Here we have to understand a crucial fact, and that is during this resurrection, the 144,000 will rise as immortals. They will have a spiritual body like Jesus had after his resurrection with which he not only could walk through walls and closed doors (John 20:19-29) but could also eat as normal human beings do (John 21:12 and 15).

But the other Christians from the time of Jesus will rise merely as humans as they were originally. This previous sentence should be understood in its correct light, and that is they will rise as mere humans with their original soul and body. But by virtue of this resurrection, their body will be devoid of any illness, ailments, defects, abnormalities, deficiencies, etc. They will have perfect bodies as the first man and woman, Adam and Eve, had (proof from the Bible given later). They will breathe, eat, and will be allowed to lead their original lives with their families. This also means that they will have all the freedom that they had earlier, and therefore, they will be capable of doing good as well as bad. The only difference between the 144,000 and the others will be that the others will not be able to walk through the doors and walls. By virtue of this resurrection, Jesus will provide the risen Christians an opportunity to know and realize their previous shortcomings, rectify them, and prepare themselves for the two special judgments of Christ. These two judgments will take place at the end of the tribulation period, just before Armageddon. They will also be given the task to prepare the Gentiles for the two special judgments by sincerely spreading the Gospel and teaching the way of the Lord. The good news is they too will be able to obtain immortality during the White Throne Judgment by living a righteous life until they appear before the judgment throne of God.

Survivors of the Tribulation

As mentioned earlier, the period of the tribulation will be three and a half years. We have to remember that the Antichrist's influence will have spread throughout the world, and therefore, the whole world will undergo suffering unheard of before. Revelation 8:6-13 and 9:1-12 gives us a graphic idea about this period. By the time the period of the tribulation and Armageddon is over, two-thirds of the population will die.

Fortunately, many of the descendents of Abraham, God's people, and the pagans living at that time will be converted into God's ways. We read this beautiful and encouraging passage in Ezekiel 36:24-28: "I will take you from every nation and country, and bring you back to your own land [Jesus's kingdom]. I will sprinkle clean water on you and make you clean from all your idols and everything else that have defiled you. I will give you a new heart and a new mind. I will take away your stubborn heart of stone and give you an obedient heart. I will put my Spirit in you and will see to it that you will follow my laws and keep my commandments I have given you. Then you will live in the land I gave your ancestors [remember, this is a prophecy, and therefore, the word land here implies God's kingdom on earth after Jesus' Millennium Rule]. You will be my people, and I will be your God."

The Two Special Judgments:

To avoid confusion, please remember that this judgment will be held a little before Armageddon. All the people living at that time, the descendents of Abraham, God's people, and the Gentiles, pagans, will face Jesus' special judgment. This judgment will be held separately, one for God's people and the other for pagans. Matthew in his Gospel gives a very clear picture of this judgment in chapter 25:31-34: "When the Son of Man comes as King and all the Angels with him, he will sit on his throne, and the people of all the nations will be gathered before him. Then he will divide them into two groups, just as a shepherd separates the sheep from the goats. He will put the righteous people on his right and the others at his left. Then the King will say to the people on his right, come that are blessed by my Father. Come and possess the Kingdom, which has been prepared for you ever since the creation of the world." This he will say to the faithful and converted God's people. These will be gathered into Jesus' army. But for the unfaithful and nonconverted God's people, he will say, "Away from me, you that are under God's curse. Away to the eternal fire which has been prepared for the devil and his angels." A word of caution, this last sentence should not be interpreted as the final condemnation. Because these condemned, as per God's plan, will be given one more opportunity to change and face the final White Throne Judgment before eternal condemnation is meted out to them by God, except the 144,000. Therefore, they will be once again sent to earth to live in the world (explained later).

A similar judgment will be held for the living pagans. Here too the righteous among them will be separated from the unrighteous. Those who did not know Christ at all will be grouped with the righteous God's people because Jesus had always known that had they been given an opportunity to know him, they would have followed him. But those among the living pagans who knew Jesus and yet did not follow him would be added among the unrighteous God's people. However, this will depend upon whether they did not follow Jesus because of their stubborn heart or they were forced and had no choice. The righteous among the living pagans, having experienced Jesus' justice firsthand, will gladly join Jesus' army and remain faithful till the end. The unrighteous pagans will also be allowed to live in the world.

The result of this judgment will be that all the rejected living God's people and the living pagans will hate the chosen ones of Jesus, and they will group together into one band and join the Antichrist for a common cause. The common cause will be to fight against Jesus and his chosen ones. Meanwhile Jesus will also form an army of the chosen ones, and God will provide them with tremendous power and skills, and both the armies will clash at Armageddon (explained earlier).

The battle will be devastating and almost totally destructive. Jesus will crush the enemy completely. Then the good Lord Jesus, instead of going back to his Father, will stay back on earth. He will establish his capital in Jerusalem and set his throne there (Isaiah 11:10 and Romans 15:12) and start building his kingdom on earth brick by brick. God inspired Prophet Amos to write, "A day is coming when I will restore the kingdom of David, which is like a house fallen into ruins. I will repair its walls and restore it. I will rebuild it and make it as it was long ago" (Amos 9: 11).

The Millennium Rule of Christ

It is wisely said that the ruled reflect the characteristics of the ruler, which means that the ruler/leader can actually shape the mind-set of his subjects albeit, good or bad. We have many examples of this in the Bible, and our history of six thousand years also bears witness to this fully.

God had a very beautiful plan for humans right from the beginning. His plan was that he wanted all people to live in peace, harmony, justice, mercy and love for one another, equality, righteousness, and brotherhood as one universal family. But Satan, through his jealousy, with the support of humans of course, derailed God's plans at the Garden of Eden. Thus, it seems that Adam and Eve and the later generations have frustrated his plans. This is because we have to remember that human beings are not puppets on a string for God. He does not control our actions and thoughts. He has given us complete freedom, so he allows us to either follow him or not. But only for six thousand years!

It is very pleasant to imagine that the period of Jesus' Millennium Rule will be a magical one, when every day Jesus will sit on his throne in Jerusalem and wave his right hand (the hand that performed so many miracles during his first presence on earth), and the Twin Towers (the World Trade Center) will reappear in New York once again, or a bridge will appear connecting the east coast of China to the west coast of Australia, or people would have obtained immortality and would be flying around like angels, somewhat like the way we are made to imagine how God's kingdom could have existed before Satan revolted and brought in chaos. But the fact of the matter is none of the magical things will happen. What actually will happen though is Jesus will set his throne at the site of King David's throne and establish Jerusalem as his capital (Isaiah 11:10; Romans 15:12). Then he will send the 144,000 immortals with the physical body like himself to different nations of the world. Some of them will be kings/leaders to govern the people under his kingship, some will be priests, preachers, and teachers to spread the gospel to the people of all caste, creed, and color, and others will hold other important positions. Since Satan has been locked in the abyss and his influence removed from the earth, the spiritual blindness of the Christians and the pagans caused by Satan and his cronies for two thousand years will gradually be lifted, and they will begin to realize that Jesus is truly the Son of God. I have mentioned only two thousand years here because we are talking about the resurrected Christians from the time of Jesus and the sheep and the goats of the first judgment as the rest of the people from the time of Adam will still be resting till the White Throne Judgment (explained later). These 144,000 will teach the living that knowing Jesus alone and following him half-heartedly is not enough to attain peace and happiness in this world and attain eternity. But it is imperative that they should totally surrender to him and God through a personal relationship. They will be taught how to yield their hearts, minds, and will to Jesus and make him the center of their lives (as how the Apostles, the prophets, and later, the canonized saints did). They will be taught how easy it is to follow the Ten Commandments and God's statutes with Jesus' support and the grace of God, which is freely available to all. They will be taught as to what Jesus meant when he told his Apostles in John 14:6, "I am the way, the truth and the life, no one can go to the Father except by Me." They will be made to understand what Apostle Paul meant when he wrote to the Galatians, "I am crucified with Christ; nevertheless I live; yet not I, but Christ lives in me; and the life which I now live in the flesh I live by the faith of the Son of God, who loved me, and gave his life for me" (Galatians 2:20). They will be taught that St. Paul was not the only one who was given this special grace during his lifetime, but all can obtain this grace because of Jesus' death on the cross (the prophets, Apostles, martyrs, and saints are proof). They will be shown that majority of God's people were blinded, and the pagans were made to live in ignorance of this grace, and therefore, Jesus couldn't be their way, their truth, and their life. In short, all the living will be given a wonderful opportunity to know the truth that Jesus is Lord of Lords and King of Kings, and eternal life can be obtained only through him. They will also be taught that surrendering to Jesus and God does not necessarily mean losing self-independence and becoming their slaves or robots or abandoning the world and living in caves high up in the mountains as the ancient monks did or become priests and nuns and live a celibate life. But all it simply means is to involve "them" totally in our lives and allow "them" to guide and lead us.

Simultaneously, the 144,000, with the help of the other righteous survivors sent to earth, will govern the people with righteousness. They will use the skills of people to build the destroyed world little by little. It will be exactly like the aftermath of the flood during Noah's time. Gradually, the world will look the way it looked before the Armageddon except that it will function according to God's laws and statutes.

Since two-thirds of the humanity would have been destroyed, there will be plenty of room for the population to increase, so humans will procreate and gradually fill the earth. There will be no sorrow, pain, and illness (as mentioned earlier). People will live longer lives as in the Old Testament. The original families will reunite and live together, and all will live in harmony, loving one another.

Jesus' Millennium Rule on earth and the way he will rule are mentioned in various places in the Bible, and it gives me sufficient reason to believe that these will surely take place. I will mention some of them in a concise way here. Jeremiah 23:5 states, "The time is coming when I will choose as King a righteous descendent of David." (Jesus is a descendent of King David through Mary his mother. Joseph, his foster father, was also a descendent of King David.) Isaiah writes, "A child is born to us a Son is given to us and he will be our ruler. He will be called, Wonderful Counselor, Mighty God, and Prince of Peace. His royal power will continue to grow; His Kingdom will always be at peace. He will rule as king David's successor" (Isaiah 9:6-7). Luke in his Gospel 1:32-33 writes, "He will make him King as his ancestor king David was." His Kingdom full of justice and peace is mentioned in the book of Prophet Micah 4:3—"He will settle disputes among nations and among the great powers near and far. They will hammer their swords into plows and their spears into pruning knives; nations will never again go to war." Micah further writes, "Everyone will live in peace among his own vineyard and fig trees and no one will be afraid." Prophet Jeremiah writes, "When He is King, the people of Judah, the Jews [spread all over the world] will be safe, and the people of Israel [descendents of Jacob] will live in peace." He will be called "Lord of our salvation" (Jeremiah 23:)]. Prophet Zechariah writes thus about long life, "I [Jesus] will return to Jerusalem, my holy city, and live there, it will be known as the faithful city, and the hill of the Lord Almighty will be called the Sacred Hill. Once again old men and women, so old that they will use canes when they walk, will be sitting in the city squares" (Zechariah 8:3-4). Isaiah writes, "People will be in good health, the blind will be able to see, and the deaf will hear. The lame will leap and dance, those who cannot speak will shout for joy [mentioned earlier]." Isaiah also wrote, "I, myself, [Jesus] will be filled with joy because of Jerusalem and her people; there will be no weeping there, no calling for help. Babies will not die in infancy, and all people will live out their life span. Those who live to be a hundred will be considered young" (Isaiah 65:19-20). Isaiah also speaks about rebuilding the destroyed world, "People will build houses and get to live in them;

they will not be used by someone else." He writes about good climate too, "Whenever you plant your crop, the Lord will send rain to make them grow and will give you rich harvest; and your livestock will have plenty of pasture. The oxen and donkeys that plow your fields will eat the first and best fodder" (Isaiah 11:5-9 and Ezekiel 47:9-19). The Lord spoke through Prophet Amos, "'The days are coming,'" says the Lord, "'when grain will grow faster than it can be harvested, and the grapes will grow faster than the wine can be made. The mountains will drip with sweet wine, and the hills will flow with it. I will bring my people back to their land. They will rebuild their ruined cities and live there; they will plant vineyards and drink the wine; they will plant gardens and eat what they grow. I will plant my people on the land I gave them, and they will not be pulled up again.' The Lord God has spoken."

About worshipping Jesus and God, Prophet Malachi writes, "Peoples from one end of the world to the other honor me. Everywhere, they burn incense to me, and offer acceptable sacrifice. All of them honor me" (Malachi 1:11). Isaiah writes, "On every new moon festival and every Sabbath people of every nation will come to worship me here in Jerusalem." Zechariah confirms, "The Lord Almighty says, the time is coming when people from many cities will come to Jerusalem. Those from one city will say to those from another, 'we are going to worship the Lord Almighty and pray for his blessings; come with us.' Many people and nations will come to Jerusalem to worship the Lord Almighty and to pray for his blessings. In those days ten foreigners [people lacking in faith] will come to one Jew [Jesus' followers sent to earth] and say, 'we want to share in your destiny, because we have heard that God is with you' and then all survivors from the nations that have attacked Jerusalem will go there each year to worship the Lord Almighty as King and to celebrate the festival of shelters" (Zechariah 8:20-23). The proof that Jesus' faithful will rule with him is mentioned in Revelation 20:4, "Then I saw thrones, and those who sat on them were given the power to judge." Jesus establishing his capital in Jerusalem is mentioned by Isaiah, "The wood of the pine, the juniper and the cypress, the finest wood from the forest of Lebanon, will be brought to rebuild you, Jerusalem, to make the temple beautiful, to make my city glorious" (Isaiah

60:13-14). These and many other passages in the Bible give us a definite idea as to how Jesus' Millennium Rule on earth will be.

There is a school of religious people that teaches amillennialism. This teaching says that Jesus' thousand year of rule on earth is just a myth. Others teach that there will not be any resurrection at all. Instead, the church will grow in power and continue to dominate the world until the final judgment—the White Throne Judgment. But, my readers, in case in spite of the many passages mentioned as proof above, some doubt still lingers in your mind, then the following passage, I am sure, will clear your doubt and make you realize that amillennialism is merely another diversion from the truth. Revelation 11:15-16 clearly says, "Then the seventh Angel blew the trumpet, and there were loud voices in heaven saying, the power to rule over the world belongs to our Lord and his Messiah and he will rule for ever and ever." Jesus himself says to John in Revelation 22:7, "'Listen,' says Jesus, 'I am coming soon, and happy are those who obey the prophetic words in the book.'" Again in Revelation 22:12, "'Listen,' Jesus says, 'I am coming soon. I will bring my reward with me to give to each one according to what he has done. I am the first and the last, beginning and the end—the alpha and omega.'"

The Second Resurrection

At the end of the Sabbath millennium—end of the seven thousandth year—however, Satan and his demons will be let loose for a short time once again (Revelation 20:7). This short time is considered to be a hundred years. Frustrated by his imprisonment of a thousand years and seeing the tremendous righteousness spread among all the nations, Satan will become ferocious like a wounded lion and will go out to all nations to try and deceive them once again. The sad thing is he will succeed in deceiving many to join him again. Once again, Satan will succeed in forming an army, and at the end of one hundred years, he will prepare to fight with Jesus again. But this time, there will not be a physical battle. Instead, God will intervene directly and send fire from above (as he did on Sodom and Gomorrah) and completely destroy Satan's army. This will be Satan's last and final attempt to gain dominion over the world because he will be thrown into the lake of fire and sulfur and destroyed forever (Revelation 20:8-10). Satan will never ever exist again. Please remember that Satan will not be burning in the fire for eternity, but it will be a one-time total burning.

Once Satan has been destroyed, the next program in God's itinerary will be the second resurrection. This second resurrection will occur at the White Throne Judgment, the final judgment. In Revelation 20:11, John says, "Then I saw a great white throne and the one who sits on it. Earth and heaven fled from his presence and were seen no more" (sign of power and authority). Then Revelation 20:12 says, "And I saw the dead, great and small alike, standing before the throne." Then Revelation 20:13 continues, "Then the sea gave up its dead. Death and the world of the dead [from the time of Adam] also gave up the dead they held." Going back to Revelation 20:12b, we read, "Books were opened and another book was opened, the book of the living. The dead were judged according to what they had done as recorded in the books." What this passage simply means is during this judgment, all those who had not risen during the first resurrection (remember, only the Christians from Jesus' time had risen at the first resurrection) people resting from the time of Adam and those who had died during the tribulation and those who had died in the Armageddon and those who had died in the fire from above during Satan's last attempt will rise to face the White Throne Judgment, except the 144,000, plus both God's people and the pagans judged as righteous during the judgment seat of Christ who remain faithful till the last. During this judgment, books will be opened, and those facing the judgment will be judged according to what they had done as recorded in the books. We have to understand two things here. First, there are two categories of books. The first is a single book—the Bible! Yes, the Bible will be opened, and all present at the judgment will be made to understand its teachings instantaneously from beginning to end as the way Jesus had opened the minds of the two travelers on the way to Emmaus (Luke 24:13-35) after his resurrection. The purpose of this is those who survive the White Throne Judgment and taken into God's new kingdom would be full of the knowledge of God and never falter ever again for all eternity. The second category is a set of books—the book of the living in which are written the good and bad deeds of all the people during their lifetime. All facing the judgment will be judged according to their deeds during their original and subsequent life times. The names of all those who defied and rejected God in spite of repeated opportunities will be stricken off from these books, and they too will be thrown into the lake of fire and sulfur. Revelation 20:15 says, "Whoever did not have his name written in the book of the living was thrown into the lake of fire." Revelation 20:14b says, "The lake of fire is the second death." This means that there will be no more resurrection for them, no more opportunity to enter the third resurrection. The book of Revelation calls this the second death because the first death is the natural death of the human body from which all will be raised at the second resurrection. The second death is the death of only those whose names will be stricken off at the White Throne Judgment. This will be their permanent death. Fortunately, they will not suffer for all eternity as most of us are made to believe, but burnt up and disappear with Satan forever.

On the other hand, the survivors of the White Throne Judgment will enter into the third and the last resurrection.

Before we learn about the third resurrection, I think it is appropriate to know what this lake of fire and sulfur is. Is it the same as the popularly known hell? Is it a physical place and an eternal one at that? Who is existing there, and what happens to its inhabitants?

Hell

Up until recently, majority of the people (of all religions) believed that there was a physical place called hell. Honestly, I believe it was good because people were very scared of being dumped there by God and allowed to burn forever. The word hell was like a leash that kept people under control from doing wrong things to a great extent, outwardly at least. However, because of advancement in technology and the introduction of modern free society lifestyle, people not only do not believe in hell but also do not believe in evil and wrong things. Consequently, they do not believe in Satan and the demons and the evil they have caused all along and are causing now.

But as many believe, is there a physical place called hell? Will a merciful God/Father who created all humans with utmost love and care allow his favorite souls to be tortured in hell forever? It is good to remember the faithful love of the father to his prodigal son in the parable of the lost son (please read Luke 15: 11-24 to get a clear understanding of God's love for his children). Some may still say yes, God will punish at least some like Hitler, for example, to rot in hell. This is the most ridiculous concept of God. God is pure love, and because of his nature, He cannot be vengeful. Therefore, he will not allow any soul to be tortured in hell for eternity (even Hitler and the like of him will be given a second chance to learn their mistake and change). For Satan, his demons, and the rejected ones at the final White Throne Judgment, it will be a one time burning and total destruction in the blink of an eye. No pain, no suffering, no tears, no grinding of teeth—nothing. Since the soul is a spirit, it will just disappear, cease to exist, with the body. There will be no eternity for them, only instant burning off. Some may argue that if God is so merciful, then why does he allow so much pain and suffering in the world? Well, the actual answer is it is not God who brings pain and suffering in this world. It is we who bring these upon ourselves because of our misbehavior influenced by Satan. Some may ask, if God is all-powerful, why then does he allow Satan to influence us? The answer is he has given us his statutes, and with it, he has given his teachings to follow these statutes. He has also given us an intelligent mind that can discern good from bad. In his goodness, he has not made us robots but has given us freedom and, therefore, a choice. However, he does allow pain and suffering—I am sure, with great discomfort to himself of course—in the world not to punish us but out of love to open our minds and hearts and bring us back to him. This logic may sound funny and/or stupid but ask anyone who has turned to God after great sufferings, and they will tell you exactly what I have written here.

Thus, is there a physical place called as hell? The answer to this question is a firm no, and the Bible bears witness to this fact when it tells us that the wages of sin is death, but the gift of God is eternal life through Jesus

Christ our Lord (Romans 6:23). Thus, as mentioned in an earlier chapter, immortality is not our automatic inheritance even for the righteous ones, but immortality is a gift granted graciously by God, first to the 144,000 at the first resurrection and to others after the White Throne Judgment. Hell is a manmade concept. I sincerely believe that using the word eternal as in eternal damnation is wrong because there is no eternal damnation, only instant damnation. The word eternal should be used only as in eternal life because all the survivors of the White Throne Judgment will for sure have eternal life with Jesus, God, and with one another.

So now the question is how did this hell concept come into existence at all? The answer is it came into existence through the imagination of one famous person by the name of Dante Alighieri. He wrote a poem describing the totally corrupt political situation of his time many centuries ago. In the poem, he described a large pit with nine descending stages of fire in which the corrupt politicians—he considered them as sinners—would be punished. The top, being the mildest, was for the lesser corrupt politicians, and the bottommost, being the most severe, was for the totally corrupt politicians. He called the lower stages inferno in which, these most corrupt politicians (sinners) would be tortured by fire. We all know that anything very famous people do say or write gets caught up in the society easily. But this concept somehow got caught up even in the religious society as well. This, I believe, was probably because the concept gave tremendous power to the religious authorities to keep people under control. So that is how hell was actually created.

Similarly, there is no mention of Purgatory in the Bible anywhere. However, the church has drilled this concept too in the minds of the faithful. Therefore, prayers and Eucharistic celebrations (Mass) are offered at a price for the souls to rest in peace. Ironically, the truth is that they would rest in peace even otherwise because God has planned it to be that way until the last judgment and second resurrection. The church seems to have overlooked the truth or forgotten by design to teach that salvation and condemnation is self-achievable. That is, no one else can send one to hell or to heaven; one can attain either one on his/her own free will alone. The choice is entirely for the individual to make while he/she is alive.

Once dead, nothing, and no one except God, can save or obtain peace to the dead, neither prayers nor Eucharistic celebrations. That is why God, in his mercy, has made provision through subsequent resurrections.

Thus the word hell mentioned in many places in the Bible should not be interpreted as a physical place that is circulating around, but it is to be understood as one-time lake of fire and sulfur mentioned in the book of Revelation. There is a passage in Revelation 20:10 that could lead to some confusion. It says, "Then the devil who deceived them was thrown into the lake of fire and sulfur, where the beast and the false prophets had already been thrown; and they will be tormented day and night forever and ever." John is not talking about hell here, but he is describing in a symbolic way (his vision), how Satan and his cronies would suffer for a thousand years in the abyss (not hell). The thousand years of captivity will surely appear as eternity in hell to them.

A word of caution! This explanation should not be taken literally to mean that because there is no physical hell, we are free to do whatever we want. Not at all, but rather it should be taken merely as an explanation to the misconception/misunderstanding that is circulating around. It is not intended to make people believe in "no hell, no punishment, therefore no problem—live as you like." That sort of living would be an unfortunate felony because we have to remember that there will be a judgment and that the wicked will be punished.

Now that we have taken the tour of Hades and hell, I think it is time to meet the ghosts who are believed to cause terrible harm and pain in the lives of people.

Ghosts

While some religions do not talk much about ghosts and thus leave their followers in a limbo, others actually promote the belief in their existence, and the innocent and ignorant followers not only accept this belief but also cause others to accept it. Besides, authors churn out such realistic ghost stories that the spellbound reader is left hanging in the air whether to accept it as true or not. Movies are not far behind. With the help of modern technology, we are bombarded with such graphic and true-to-life themes that the audiences are left dazed watching them, and some end up having sleepless nights.

The result of all this is that majority is mesmerized into believing that ghosts do exist. The sad thing is that this innocence and ignorance is being exploited by religious heads and vested individuals for selfish motives and financial gain. Therefore, I believe it is time for true light to be shed on this topic so that many, if not all, will find relief from exploitation. So the question is do ghosts exist at all? The answer is they *do not* because *they cannot*. Only people with a rational mind combined with a fairly good knowledge of the scripture will be able to accept this truth.

The Bible clearly states that once a person dies, his body decays and the soul rests in Hades until it is either raised during the first resurrection or at the final judgment. God alone, being the owner of all, has the power to raise both body and soul on these occasions. Therefore, no other authority on earth, above the earth, under the earth, or in the sea can raise, invoke, or cause souls to appear from their resting place. Neither can they come back to earth even temporarily on their own to perform any task. This is because the spirits of the dead people have no power whatsoever; God has not given them the power that he had given the angels. Consequently, it can be firmly confirmed that all the talk about the troubled spirits roaming the earth, haunting people, taking revenge, and performing harmful deeds is nonsense.

Yet we have unlimited proof that people have been haunted and troubled. So what is the explanation? The explanation is very simple if only we remember that the devil and his demons exist and that they have retained their power given to them by God. With that power, they not only can appear in any shape and form but also can do anything they want, except take the life of a person. However, they can induce one to commit suicide. Having read the above, my reader may have realized that the people who claim to invoke the dead spirits are in fact invoking the devil or his demons, depending on the gravity of the situation. We have to remember here that many of these people are pretenders/fakes who are out there to cheat people and make money. But there are individual people and cults who can actually appease the devil and or demon, but to do that, they have to totally surrender their heart, soul, mind, and body and become their slaves, a truth that may be hard to digest.

I believe the incident I am going to narrate below from the Bible gives substance to what I have mentioned above. In the Gospel of Luke 8:26-30, we read that Jesus and his disciples sail over to the territory of Gerasa that is across the lake from Galilee. There they meet a man possessed with demons. The moment he sees Jesus, he throws himself at the feet of Jesus and shouts, "Jesus Son of the most high God! What do you want with me? I beg you, don't punish me." So Jesus asks him, . . . What is your name?" "My name is Mob," he answered because many demons had gone into him (*mob* means "many"). Jesus, out of pity, heals him by driving the demons into a herd of pigs that were feeding on the hillside close by. To understand this incident clearly in its true light, we have to realize that the person did not know Jesus at all, and therefore, it was not the person who was uttering the words, but the demons possessing the man were speaking through him because they knew Jesus very well. That is why the moment they faced Jesus, they were frightened and begged him not to punish them because they knew he had the power to do so.

Observe carefully the name used here. It is many demons, and *not* spirits of many dead people. This clearly points out that only the devil or his cronies can possess people and perform harmful tasks, and not the spirits (ghosts) of the dead people.

However, man can take consolation and courage by knowing the truth that though the devil and the demons have retained all the power given to them by God and with that they can seemingly do anything, they cannot wield their power over humans unless we succumb/surrender to them either through ignorance, fright, deception, detachment from God, arrogance, or desperation. We have to know, believe, and accept the truth that they have no power over us because we are made in the image of God, and therefore, we have God's Spirit and grace in us no matter which religion we belong to. Besides, Jesus has won victory over Satan (for all humans) by dying on the cross, and by virtue of this death, he has obtained power from God for us to crush Satan and his demons.

How then do some people drive the devil from people possessed by it? The simple answer is people do not drive the devil away. Only God has the power to do so. But God does use specially anointed people as his instruments to carry on this task [read Mark 16: 17-18]. This can be seen in the parable where Jesus said to the Pharisees and the crowd after he drove the demon out of another man on a different occasion in Luke 11: 16: "Others wanted to trap Jesus, so they asked him to perform a miracle to show that God approved of him. But Jesus knew what they were thinking, so he said to them, 'Any country that divides itself into groups which fight each other will not last very long; a family divided against itself falls apart. *So if Satan's kingdom has groups fighting each other, how can it last?* [italics mine] You say that I drive out demons because Beelzebul [Satan] gives me the power to do so. If this is how I drive them out, how do your followers drive them out? Your own followers prove that you are wrong! No, *it is rather by means of God's power that I drive out demons,* and this proves that the Kingdom of God has already come to you.'" Thus only special people filled with God's grace and power can drive the devil or his demons, and they have to do so strictly for the benefit of others, and not for their own benefit in any way or else their power will be taken away from them.

The Third Resurrection

The third resurrection will actually be a moving on from mortality to immortality because after the second resurrection, there will not be death. God will transform every survivor of the White Throne Judgment into immortal beings, not like Casper the Friendly Ghost but like Jesus after his resurrection. St. Paul explains this beautifully in 1 Corinthians 15:51-55: "Listen to this secret truth [hidden to the blinded people of this age], we shall not die [after the second resurrection], but when the last trumpet [seventh] sounds, we shall all be changed in an instant, as quickly as the blinking of an eye. For, when the trumpet sounds the dead will be raised never to die again, and we shall all be changed. For what is mortal must be changed into what is immortal; what will die must be changed into what cannot die. So when this takes place, the mortal has been changed into immortal, then the scripture will come true. Death is destroyed; victory is complete! Where, death, is your victory? Where, death, is your power to hurt?"

Chapter IX

What Will Happen after This? The New Heaven and the New Earth

The whole of chapter 21 and chapter 22:1-5 of Revelation explains what and how the New Heaven and New Earth will be. But with all the propaganda going on about the nonexistence of God, the universe being created by a big bang, and the scientists desperately trying to prove the theory of evolution, can the religious minded prove that there is a heaven at all? If hard physical proof is asked for, the answer is an outright no. But the existence of the New Heaven and New Earth can be explained logically and can be proven with the help of the Bible.

Religious people believe that God has no beginning and no end and that he created the universe. Therefore, obviously, God must be dwelling somewhere. Since he is a spirit being, he does not need a physical place to live, which means he has no limitations and, therefore, can exist in the entire universe including the earth. That is why God inspired prophet Isaiah to write, "The Lord says, 'Heaven is my throne, and earth is my footstool. What kind of house [dwelling place] then, could you build for me to live in [to contain]? I, myself, created the universe'" (Isaiah 66:1-2a). This clearly indicates that God lives everywhere, and therefore, heaven is everywhere even on earth, especially in the human heart. Sadly, we have forgotten that God had put Adam in the Garden of Eden, which was a paradise on earth, but Satan deceived him into losing it. Then according to God's plan, he gave humans his statutes and laws, observing which they could make this earth a heaven. Then when they got blinded and did not know how to follow the laws and statutes, he sent his only Son to teach them so that observing and following his teachings they could make this world a heaven again. Alas! Humans rejected all of God's plans, and for the past six thousand years, this world, instead of being a heaven, has become hell.

If God can live everywhere, then why do people look up, point toward the sky when they talk about God or pray to him? The first reason, I believe, is because, consciously or subconsciously, we acknowledge God as a supreme and powerful being who cannot dwell on earth (our level). He cannot dwell under the earth because it is the world of the dead (Hades), and a living God cannot live there anyways. So the obvious place is above somewhere in the sky. The second reason, I believe, is because of some of the incidents narrated in the Bible point to the sky like Jacob's dream at Bethel in which he sees a staircase stretching from earth to the sky on which angels were going up and down and the Lord standing beside him—apparently God too had come down the stairs from heaven (Genesis 28:12-13). Then in Luke 3:21-22 and John 1:32, we read about the heaven (sky) opening and the Holy Spirit coming down like a dove. Then again we read about Jesus ascending to heaven in the presence of his followers as mentioned in Mark 16:19 and Luke 24:50-51.

So how does one interpret the heading of Revelation 21 in the Bible "New Heaven and New Earth," and the first two passages, "I saw the holy city, the New Jerusalem coming down from heaven from God, prepared and ready, like a bride dressed to meet her husband" (Revelation 21:1-2)? The answer can be discerned easily by reading carefully and with an open mind the passages that follow from Revelation 21:3-27 and 22:1-5 while remembering at the same time that the passage is written in symbolic language. I would have liked to reproduce these passages here, but they are too long to do so. However, I would urge the readers to read these passages and continue till the end of chapter 22. The simple meaning of these passages is that after the final judgment, after Satan, his cronies, and the stubborn unconverted sinners are destroyed/burnt up in the lake of fire, the earth will be totally devoid of all evil. Therefore, God's kingdom of peace, justice, love, equality, and tranquility will descend into the hearts of all humanity and remain for all eternity literally. As mentioned earlier, the capital city will be the current physical Jerusalem, and Jesus will sit on King David's throne and rule the whole world, and the survivors of the White Throne Judgment will live with him forever. Read what God inspired Prophet Isaiah to write many centuries before John, "The Lord says I am making a new earth and new heavens [plural, explained later]. The events of the past will be completely forgotten. Be glad and rejoice forever in what I create now [new]. The Jerusalem I make [symbolizing the whole world in this text—not only the capital Jerusalem] will be full of joy, and her people will be filled with joy because of Jerusalem [Jesus' presence in capital city in this context] and her people. There will be no weeping, no calling for help, babies will no longer die in infancy and all people will live out their span of life. Those who live to be hundred will be considered young" (Isaiah 65:17-20a). Isaiah was also inspired to write, "He will rule his people with justice and integrity, wolves and sheep will live together in peace, and leopards will lie down with young goats. Calves and lion cubs will feed together, and little children will take care of them. Cows and bears will eat together, and their calves and cubs will lie down in peace. Lions will eat straw as cattle do. Even a baby will not be harmed if it plays near a poisonous snake. On Zion, God's holy hill, there will be nothing harmful or evil. The land will be as full of knowledge of the Lord as the seas are full of water" (Isaiah 11:5-9).

Dear reader, this is the New Heaven and New Earth that we are promised and for which all humanity is created. Heaven will be on earth itself. At that time, heaven and earth will not be considered as two separate entities but will be combined and dwell together. What a glorious future to hope and work hard for, more than any worldly materialistic goal. That is why when the Apostles asked Jesus to teach them to pray, Jesus taught them the Lord's prayer, "Our Father, who art in heaven, hallowed be thy name, *thy Kingdom come thy will be done, on earth as it is in heaven* [italics mine]. Give us this day our daily bread and forgive us our trespasses, as we forgive those who trespass against us and do not lead us into temptation, but deliver us from evil."

Now, what was that "the new heavens" I had mentioned earlier? The word new heavens mentioned in the passage of Isaiah 65:17 talks not only about the heaven on earth but also speaks about the whole universe. God's words in the Bible promise us that those who gain eternal life after the White Throne Judgment will inherit all things and rule over it. We can grasp this truth by carefully studying and adding up the following passages of the Bible. St. Paul was inspired to encourage the Galatians, "To redeem those who were under the law, so that we might become God's sons. To show that you are his sons, God sent the Spirit [Holy Spirit] of his Son [Jesus] into our hearts the Spirit that cries out, 'Father, my Father.' So then, you are no longer a slave but a son. And since you are his son, God will give you [as inheritance] all that he has for his sons" (Galatians 4:5-7). St. Paul has also written somewhat the same thing to the Romans in chapter 8 verse 17. Many centuries before, God inspired even King David to write, "When I look at the sky which you have made, at the moon and the stars which you have set in their places, what is man that you think of him, mere man, that you care for him? Yet you made him inferior only to yourself, you crowned him with glory and honor. You appointed him ruler over everything you made; you placed him over *all creation [italics mine]*" (Psalm 8:3-6). Can we really comprehend the depth of this Psalm and the above-mentioned passages and the meaning contained in it? The love of God depicted in it and the blessings that God has freely made available to us? As mentioned earlier, St. Paul tells us that God's love is unconditional, and he has made us even above the angels and given us the authority to judge them.

"Over everything you made" means "dominion over all things." The passage clearly tells us that because of Jesus' death on the cross, he has redeemed us and has transformed us into the sons of God and Jesus' brothers and coheirs in Jesus' inheritance, which is the whole universe. Jesus confirmed this to his followers just before he ascended into heaven, "I have been given all authority in heaven and on earth" (Matthew 28: 18).

Therefore, together with Jesus, the survivors of the White Throne Judgment will dominate the whole universe. The limited scientific knowledge that we struggle to gain little by little now will be opened and expanded into limitless knowledge of God. Since all will possess eternal life, all will be able to live over the entire universe (the current desire to colonize the space and seeking out other living things in the space could be a genetically embedded trait in us by God, and the current achievements in the space could be a prelude or foretaste of what is in store in the future). Am I hallucinating? I am sure I am not because the Greek word for all things used by St. Paul to the Hebrews 2:8 and the Romans 8:32 is panta, which means "the universe." This shows that God did not create the universe because he was a magician and fancied it or because he had nothing else to do. He created it because he had an eternally stupendous plan. In this stupendous plan, he planted humans only on earth, initially. But later, he would allow them to inherit the whole universe! Unfortunately, Adam's disobedience delayed the whole process. Yet fortunately, all is not lost because of Jesus. As far as I am concerned, this rules out the big bang theory for me.

When I watch space programs on TV, I feel very happy and emotional to think that one day I too would be whizzing around the universe for real as part of my reward, provided of course I am elected as one of the survivors of the White Throne Judgment. I am working toward it very hard and very sincerely and have left the rest to God.

Chapter X

The Book of Revelation Revealed

Readers are encouraged here to remember that the book of Revelation is not a doomsday book as many preach it to be. But it is a book of encouragement and promise of a glorious future that is awaiting all humans. This glorious future, however, can only be obtained by studying the book carefully and following the teachings mentioned therein meticulously.

At this juncture, I believe that it is necessary to simplify the book of Revelation. For many centuries, many have tried to explain this book positively as well as negatively. The church has been explaining it positively but not entirely, and negatively by people with vile interests. Honestly, it is a very confusing book, so I was told not to read it until I was quite familiar first with the New Testament and then with the Old Testament with its various prophecies by different prophets. Many of my friends also told me that they too were given same instructions. I personally believe that this is an excellent advise because this book can be properly understood only by the humble and simple-minded people who have the Spirit of God and absolute faith in his existence, in his involvement in human affairs, his unconditional love, mercy and forgiveness, and his single desire to grant eternal life with him to all creation. This total confidence in God comes only after studying the Bible in its true light. This true light, the light of the Holy Spirit, begins to pour on us gradually as we continue to study the

Bible diligently. From the beginning of the world, as we may have realized by now, these gifts were and are freely available to one and all. But as mentioned earlier, majority of the people have knowingly or unknowingly, freely or forcefully, rejected them because the Evil One has blinded them. "'This people will listen and listen, but not understand; they will look and look, but not see, because their minds are dull, and they stopped their ears, and have closed their eyes. Otherwise, their eyes would see, their ears would hear, their minds would understand, and they would turn to me,' says God, 'and I would heal them'" (Matthew 13:14-15). Also read Isaiah 6:9-10. Mind you, this blindness is not the work of humans alone; in fact, the major contribution is from the Evil One. He is so subtle and cunning that humans become his prey easily even without realizing it, sort of unawares. However, we can have courage and live in confidence with the knowledge that Satan or his cronies cannot force us to do evil. They cannot make us do things we do not want to do. They on their own cannot take us to be burnt up. They need our total cooperation. We alone are responsible for our own destiny. They can only cunningly coax us, cleverly cheat us, and thus by manipulation, lead us into sin, into their trap. Once there, they can make us blind and stubborn so that it is next to impossible to release oneself from their trap. Their companionship can only lead to destruction. But the blinded person fails to realize this till disaster strikes. It is usually at this point that man feels abandoned and lost. Yet even at this point, the person fails to recognize that it is the work of the devil, and instead of blaming the devil and correcting himself, the person starts blaming God. Fortunately, the merciful God who knows our weaknesses steps in without fail with his grace. He provides many clues of his grace and sends his Holy Spirit to understand this grace. He then expects the person to change and draw closer to him. He even performs miracles sometimes to draw the person close to him. Unfortunately, many, if not all, stubbornly and willingly discard this grace and lead a miserable life, even commit suicide.

I repeat what I mentioned at the beginning of this book, and that is I am a simple-hearted man and that this book is written for the simple-hearted people like me. Therefore, I will try to explain the book of Revelation in a simple way, the simple way that I have understood it, and I have been led and inspired to write.

One of the reasons why the book of Revelation is difficult to understand, I believe, is because the reader may ignorantly misunderstand that John has compiled many visions into one book. But the fact is the book of Revelation is a single vision with series of events seen by John. Also, many may not know that Jesus himself revealed them through symbolic revelations, and therefore, John had to write them symbolically as well. The purpose was twofold. First, only the Christians who were being persecuted at that time were given this message, and they were the only ones who were to know its meaning. The message was meant to encourage them to remain steadfast in their faith and hope. It did help them a great deal because people at that time believed that Jesus would come again within their lifetime (as promised) and relieve them of their misery. That was a message of hope and of salvation. However Jesus' delay in coming began to turn this very important message into a nonevent, and the later generation lost its essence and meaning (understanding). The result is, as I mentioned earlier, the Evil One had an easy opportunity to deceive most people.

The second purpose was that it was a prophecy for the future as well, a prophecy to be understood by all people only toward the end time. This is because many events had to take place during the end of the end time, which were prophesied in the prophecy (we have discussed them in detail, both through the eyes of the Bible and history). If we care to look around at the current events that are taking place around the world and recognize them in the light of all the events that have already taken place according to this prophecy, instead of ignoring them as natural events, we can see the inevitable eventuality.

Another reason for difficulty in understanding the book of Revelation is like a symphony, the themes are repeated and also are placed (seemingly) haphazardly. So many times, it is difficult to weave them in a sequence.

Another reason is because of the many symbols used therein, like for example the beasts, the seven churches, the seven seals, the seven horses, the seven trumpets, the two witnesses, the plagues, the bowls of anger, the famous prostitute, the wedding feast of the lamb, the rider on the white horse, etc. Though they have a specific meaning and purpose, they are difficult to understand and connect them to specific events by a casual reader unless explained by someone who is well versed in the actual truth.

The fourth reason, and I think an important one, is we have seen that the book of Revelation has a direct connection with the book of Daniel. But since the book of Daniel was written many centuries before the events actually occurred, while the book of Revelation was written by John when many of the events prophesied by Daniel had already taken place and only the end was awaited, a casual or ignorant reader may be unable or fail to notice the connection between these two prophecies, one of the Old Testament and the other of the New Testament.

The fifth reason is the Revelation (vision) is in symbolic language. The reader may not have been fully informed or taught how to interpret them and connect them to historical events and people (the characters who played the part in it).

Therefore, in my book, I have tried to incorporate all these shortcomings, albeit as clearly and as briefly as possible so that my readers may become familiar with them and understand them better.

The cream of the theme of the book of Revelation as already discussed is that all the events would take place during the end time. I have already explained some of the characters and the series of events that would take place. I will now try to explain the symbols used in the book of Revelation.

A. The Seven Churches of Asia

Although John was addressing the seven churches of Asia that existed during his time, we have to remember that the prophecy was also for the future. Therefore, the seven churches refer to the seven eras that the church would pass through from its inception till the second coming of Jesus. A careful combined study of the situation mentioned in the Bible regarding each church mentioned therein and the history of the church up till now will show us the connection and the truth (readers are recommended to read books on church history). For example, the message to the Church of Ephesus indicates the period of the beginning of the church. "I know how hard you have worked how patient you have been." All Christians know how hard the Apostles had worked and the sufferings and death they endured to establish the church. On the other hand, the message to the Church of Laodicea clearly indicates our time (the seventh and the last era before the coming of Christ), "I know what you have done; I know that you are neither cold nor hot. How I wish you were either one or the other." We have to remember that Jesus himself addressed these words to John. Don't we see the truth of this prophecy in the current "neither cold nor hot" religious condition of the church?

B. The Scroll and the Lamb of Chapter 5

The scroll in this chapter refers to the book of the living that would be opened at the White Throne Judgment. The chapter clearly states that the Lamb, who is Jesus, as we all know, is the only one who has the worthiness, permission, and authority to take it from God the Father and open it to judge those facing the judgment.

C. The Seals of Chapter 6

There are seven seals and four horses. They refer to the seven events that will take place during the three and a half years just before Jesus' coming, which will culminate in Armageddon (read the incidents mentioned when the sixth seal is opened). The rider on the white horse of Revelation 6:2 should not be mistaken for Jesus because the rider mentioned there has a bow, and not a sword and only one crown. This rider, the passage says, will ride out as a conqueror to conquer. This rider should be understood as Satan's representative, the Antichrist. On the other hand, the rider on the white horse of Revelation 19 can be easily recognized as Jesus because verse 11 calls him Faithful and True and introduces him beautifully till the end of verse 15. Then verse 16 calls him King of Kings and Lord of Lords. The fact that Jesus will break open the seals indicate that he himself will allow these events to occur.

D. The 144,000 People of Chapter 7

We have discussed about them earlier. Please note that they are mentioned again in chapter 14 as well, and they are the same.

E. The Enormous Crowd of Chapter 7:9

These are the survivors of the Armageddon. Between the sixth and the seventh seal, three and a half years will lapse, and at the end of this period, the seventh seal will be opened, which will herald the descent of Jesus on Mount Zion (Olives) in all glory, majesty, and power. The seven angels blowing seven trumpets and the seven pestilences described are a symbolic way of showing the frightful things that will take place. The first five trumpets describe the cosmic occurrences because of which one-third of the living creatures will die. The sixth trumpet describes the assembling of the huge army from east, west, north, and south for the final battle of Armageddon when another one-third of the living creatures will die, making it two-thirds (as prophesied and described earlier). Even by casually reading Revelation 9:13-19, we can understand how clearly John has described modern war equipment, albeit symbolically.

F. The Little Scroll of Chapter 10

Although it is not mentioned anywhere in the Bible, I truly believe that on this scroll was written the exact year, the month, the day, and the hour Jesus would physically descend on Mount Zion. Since Jesus revealed everything else about the end time to John, I don't think Jesus would be unfair and deprive John of this important information. Jesus loved John dearly during his life on earth, and therefore, he would not withhold this crucial information from him. But John was not allowed to write it down. Instead, an angel wrote it, and then John was allowed to read it, eat it, and keep secret what he had read. This is because of what Jesus had said to his disciples, "No one knows, however, when that day and the hour will come, neither the angels in heaven nor the Son. The Father alone knows"

(Matthew 24:36). Readers are encouraged to read till verse 44. What Jesus meant when he said "nor the Son" in the Gospel of Matthew was that, at that time when he said this, he was in human nature and so God the Father had not revealed the exact time to him yet. But at the time Jesus revealed it to John, Jesus was with the Father and so Jesus knew the time, which I believe, he must have revealed to John.

Stepping back to Noah's time, we can see the similarity of events. God had warned the people living during Noah's time of the impending flood (for one hundred years from the time God asked Noah to build the ark till the flood came) but no one believed. Everyone went about doing his or her own things because everything seemed normal. So there was no panic. Similarly, we too are being warned repeatedly, but unfortunately, majority of us console ourselves by believing that this is all the work of nature. We forget that nature also is the work of God. In our arrogance, we do not want to accept the fact that God does not speak to us directly these days, but he can and is speaking through his creation. This is because the Evil One has made us so utterly dumb, immune, and blind that we fail to recognize the signs, and therefore, there is no panic and no sign of change in people's attitude. Tragically, this will go on till the final disaster strikes, and then when it does, God only save us.

I say this because, Jesus tells his Apostles in Matthew 24:37-39, "The coming of the Son of Man will be like what happened in the time of Noah. In the days before the flood people ate and drank, men and women married, up to the very day Noah went into the boat; yet they did not realize what was happening until the flood came and swept them all away. That is how it will be when the Son of Man will come." And then he warns them not to take his words lightly by saying, "Heaven and earth will pass away but my words will never pass away." I believe that, this is one warning we should take seriously because we are in the same situation now as people were at the time of Noah.

G. The Two Witnesses of Chapter 11

Prophet Zechariah introduced these two witnesses to us many centuries before John was even born. In chapter 4 of his book, like in the book of Revelation, he calls them two olive trees beside the lamp stand (4:3), and later he tells us that they are the two men whom God has chosen and anointed to serve him, the Lord of the earth (4:14). These witnesses (prophets) will be specially chosen from among the righteous people of that time. They will be specially anointed to hold the faithful together and carry on God's work during the three and a half years of tribulation when the Antichrist will ban the daily and set up the awful horror. But they will be killed. However, after three and a half days, they will be raised and taken into heaven. Verse 10 in that chapter says, "The people of the earth will be happy because of the death of these two. They will celebrate and send presents to each other, because those two Prophets brought much suffering upon mankind." What the passage means is that the followers of the Antichrist will celebrate the death of the two prophets because these two witnesses would strongly and boldly resist the Antichrist and manage to hold the faithful together, and therefore, they will be martyred. But when they are raised after three and a half days, many of the Antichrist's followers will be converted.

H. The Seventh Trumpet of Chapter 11:15

Please take note that this chapter is meant not only to be taken symbolically but also literally because this event will actually (visibly) take place when Jesus descends on Mount Zion (Mount of Olives). Please read this very important chapter before proceeding.

I. The Woman and the Dragon of Chapter 12

The woman symbolizes the church, and the dragon the Satan. After the assumption of the two witnesses of chapter 11, the church would be without support, and Satan would try to destroy it. But God will send his angels to safeguard the church for the remaining period of three and a half years.

We have already discussed in detail the two beasts of chapter 13. The Lamb in chapter 14 of course is Jesus, and we know who the 144,000 are.

J. The Three Angels of Chapter 14:6

The first angel (after the blowing of the seventh trumpet) will announce the arrival of Jesus. The angel will accompany Jesus with other angels with songs of praise. But the second and the third angel will announce the fall of Satan, the fall of Jerusalem (Jerusalem is called Babylon here because the Antichrist is paralleled with ancient Nimrod whose capital was Babylon), and the punishment that would await those who died serving the Antichrist. But we have to remember that these too will be raised at the White Throne Judgment and given one more chance to change during the one hundred years when Satan will be let loose. However, if they do not change, they will be punished.

K. The Harvest of the Earth

Sadly, this harvest speaks of the slaughter that would take place during the Armageddon. Similarly, chapters 15 and 16 speak of the terrible plagues, pestilences, and calamities that would befall the earth during the three and a half years.

L. The Famous Prostitute

The famous prostitute is of course the city of Jerusalem, but this chapter is not talking about the physical city but its people and the lifestyle they have been leading during their entire history and the lifestyle they would lead under the rule of the Antichrist. It also indicates the fate the city and its ruler will meet at the end. Chapter 18 explains this vividly.

In the light of the background I have given so far and also the discussions we have had about the events earlier, it will be easy for my readers to understand chapter 19 onward.

Chapter XII

Is Jesus God?

Let me rephrase this question. Was Jesus God before he came to earth as man? Was he God and man when he was on earth? Is he God now? Will he be God when he comes again? Will he rule as the King of Kings of the universe?

Truly, I believe you have to answer these questions yourself in the light of all that you have read in this book. Therefore, I leave it up to you. However, I feel the following references will help you to a great extent in this task.

1. "Before the world was created, *the word [italics mine]* already existed; he [Jesus] was with God [Father], and he was the same as God. From the very beginning the Word [Jesus] was with God. Through him [Jesus] God [Father] made all things, not one thing in all creation was made without him" (John 1:1-3).
2. He will be born in Bethlehem in the land of Judah (Micah 5:2, Matthew 2:1, and Matthew 5-6).
3. He will be the Son of God, for he will be born not from flesh but by the power of the Holy Spirit to a virgin (Psalm 2:7, Isaiah 7:14, Isaiah 8:29, Luke 1:28-35, and Luke 3:22).
4. He will be called Immanuel, which means "God with us" (Isaiah 7:14 and Matthew 1:23).

5. "Your way will be prepared by a prophet" (Isaiah 40:3-5, Matthew 3:3, Mark 1:1-3, and Luke 1:76-77]. John the Baptist was sent to prepare Jesus' way.
6. He will be called Wonderful Counselor, Mighty God, Eternal Father, Prince of Peace (Isaiah 9:6).
7. "He will be a Mighty Savior, a descendent of King David and will rule with justice and peace forever" (Isaiah 9:7, Ezekiel 37:24-28, Daniel 7:14, Luke 1:32, and Luke 1:69).
8. He proved his divinity while he was alive during the transfiguration (Matthew 17:1-8, Mark 9:2-8, Luke 9:28-36, and 2 Peter 1:17-18).

These and many other passages prove beyond doubt that Jesus was God, yet he took the form of a man (to resemble and be like us) and lived for thirty-three and a-half years with the humans and died like a human. But he rose and ascended to heaven on his own, which he could do because he is God, the second person of the Trinity. The proof of his resurrection and ascension is mentioned in the Gospel of Mark 16:19 and Luke 24:50-53.

Now we know that Judaism was the dominant religion of the Middle Eastern world in the ancient days. We also know that God the Father, through Abraham, founded Judaism, and Christianity is its offshoot that came on the world scene about two thousand years ago. Islam is its other offshoot, which came into being about 1,500 years ago. We also know that Judaism, Christianity, and Islam are the three dominant religions of the western, Middle Eastern, and even some of the eastern countries now, and that they came from the same root Abraham/Judaism. That is why Abraham is called the father of these three religions.

Thus by virtue of this fact, the Jews and the Moslems are aware, through the prophecies mentioned in their scriptures, that Jesus is the Son of God, the promised Messiah. They cannot contradict this fact. Unfortunately, the Jews did not walk in God's ways and give heed to the scriptures in the right spirit. Therefore, by the time Jesus arrived, they had become arrogant, selfish, self-deceptively superior, and self-deceptively self-righteous, and so they refused to acknowledge and accept Jesus as the Messiah, the promised Son of God. They are still waiting for the Messiah to come. Fortunately, their eyes will be opened when Jesus comes on earth just before Armageddon. Similarly, the Moslems are also aware of the identity of Jesus.

Many of my readers may be surprised to note that the only woman mentioned by name in the Koran, the sacred book of the Moslems is the Virgin Mary, mother of Jesus (Miriam/Mary). The annunciation by Angel Gabriel and Mother Mary's virgin conception is also mentioned therein. A word of clarification here, what I have written above is for comparative observation only.

But the most surprising and awesome evidence about the Old Testament and about Jesus I encountered was in the sacred books of the Hindus.

The Hindus have four sacred books called Vedas. Among them, Rigveda is accepted to be the foremost, original, and supreme. Besides these four, there are other sacred books, which are considered as subsidiaries. Until Sanskrit language evolved around 1500 BCE, these were primarily kept alive through memory by chanting (like the Psalms by the Jews/Christian monks). Like how the Hebrew language originated in and around the Jordan River, the Sanskrit language evolved and flourished around River Kubah (Kabul) in Afghanistan and advanced until the bank of the Indus River. The logic we can deduce from this is that the people of the east could well be the descendents of Noah who drifted toward the east during the time of population expansion. Many indications in the Vedas point to this. The Vedic hymns were revelations received by various sages (prophets) after deep meditation of many years.

Let us dwell on some of the almost word-to-word similarities in the Rigveda and the Bible. In the first book of Prathisargaparvam, chapter 4, verse 28, we read:

Indriyani damithwa
Yehyaathmadhyaana parayana:
thasmad Aadama naamaasou
pathnee Havyavathee_Smritha"

"Aadama [Adam] and his Pathnee [wife] Havyavathee [Eve] are born with all virtues, complete control of the senses and the spiritual forbearance of the mind. God creates a captivating paradise and gifts it to Aadama to live happily. Aadama reaches beneath the tree of sin in the garden, eats its forbidden fruit, tempted by Kali [Satan] disguised as a snake."

The names of the descendents of Adam, especially Moosa [Moses] and the faith he will spread over the world right up to the time of Jesus, can be identified in the books of Rigveda. Let me give a few names here. Aadama [Adam] and Havyavathee's [Eve] son is Shwethanama [Seth]; his son is Anoohan [Enoch], Keenashan [Keenan], Mahallalan [Mahallalel], Viradan [Jared], Hanukan [Enoch], Manochillan [Methuselah], Lomakan [Lamach], and Newhan [Noah]. Jesus is called Easa Maseeh, and it is mentioned that he will be born in the land of Hunadesha. We all know that Easa Maseeha—Messiah—is the Hebrew name for Jesus. It is mentioned that the King Shakapathi of Hunadesha meets with a man clad with white clothes, and they have this conversation.

Ko bhavaanithi tham praaha
Sahovaachamudaanwitha:
Eshaputhram cha maam vidhi
Kumaaree garbha sambahavam
Aham Eesa Maseeha nama:

"'May I know who you are?' the king asks and with joy that man replied, 'Know that I am the Son of God. I am born in the womb of a virgin. Easa Maseeha is my well-known name.'"

Besides, in the tenth book, apart from the name of God Almighty, there is a mention about a man, the first and only born Son of God. He is called there as Prajapathy. "Prajapathy, the Son of God comes to this world at the appointed time. He will travel around teaching and preaching mankind about good and evil, what is good and what is not. Those who accept his advice and obey his teachings he will offer peace and prosperity in this life and salvation at the time of death. After his time of redeeming mankind, at the end of his specified period on earth, he will get sacrificed."

Further in verse seven of chapter 90 of the tenth book, it is mentioned thus, "At the time of sacrifice he will be tightly tied to a wooden sacrificial post, using iron nails by hand and feet, he will bleed to death and on the third day he will regain his life in a resurrection." How precisely described!

This Prajapathi is also known as Hiranyagarba. In the 121 verse of the first hymn of the tenth volume of Rigveda, see how Jesus Christ is described as the creator of all.

Hiranyagarba: samavarthathaagre
Bhuuthasya jaath: pathireka aaseeth
Sadaadhaara Prudhwivim dyaamuthemam
Kasmai devaaya havisha vidhemam.

"Hiranya Garba [Prajapathi] the first-born was born to the Holy Spirit [Paramathma] before Genesis. Upon birth he became the one and only God to the Universe comprising the skies, stars, earth and the seas. He rules the endless firmament and the whole of the earth. We please this deity, who is called 'Kan' affectionately, with offering in sacrifice."

We find a clear mention of the flood event too. "God warns Newhan [Noah] in a dream of the impending flood and asks him to build a boat and take refuge with his whole family. The floodgates of the sky opened and it rained for forty days and forty nights. All the seas and the earth were covered with water. Only Newhan and his family survived. By their prayer the flood receded and was gone."

Further, just look at this narrative: "When the era of Kali [Satan] has reached 3000 years Esa Maseeha will appear in the land of Huna." To the Hindus, this (current) year will be 5095th year of Kali [Satan's era], which coincides with the birth of Jesus two thousand years ago and the Christian belief of six thousand years of Satan's rule (only a few years remaining). These are but a few of the similarities I have mentioned here, between the Hindu scripture and the Bible, but there are many more.

The question one may be tempted to ask is if so much is written about Jesus, and so many corroborating proofs are available, then why don't the Hindus accept Christianity? There are three reasons I can think of. First, as until recently the Bible was not available to ordinary people, the sacred books of the Hindus are not easily accessible to all Hindus because translations from Sanskrit are not easily available. Thus, only the priestly clan and scholarly hierarchy know these similarities.

Secondly, like the Jews and Moslems who know the truth yet are reluctant to harmonize the three religions, the Hindu hierarchy is reluctant to unite under one banner.

Thirdly, the ordinary people who are born into the religion are made to believe that theirs is the true and only religion, and therefore, they are comfortable to carry on. And even if they are enlightened, they may not be willing to go through the hassle of a change.

What about the other major religion of the Orient—Buddhism? Since it originated in India, established by a Hindu king whose name was Siddhartha Gautama Buddha, I am inclined to believe that their sacred books too have the mention of Jesus. I was watching a documentary on Buddhism on the TV recently, and to my good luck, they showed some preserved ancient documents that I believe contains mention about Jesus.

The conclusion one can arrive here is that all human beings, despite the difference in color, race, creed, and territory have all come from one original source but were dispersed and differentiated with time. Also, all religions have strong links to one another despite diversity but are kept apart by powerful, selfish, and vile human agents aided by evil spiritual forces. Thus, ordinary humans have no say in anything. For the religious leaders and their close associates, religion is no more a vehicle of peace, justice, and a way of salvation. For them, religion has become a commercial platform to browbeat followers into submission and subjection and to hoard wealth and display grandeur.

The consequence is that religious leaders and the way they run their institutions have become the main cause to a great extent for religious disillusionment and man's detachment from God. Considering this helpless situation of humans, can we blame ourselves? No, to a great degree because to see is to believe, as they say. Man cannot see God, but man can see the administration of God-created institutions and the morals of God's appointed people who run these institutions. Unfortunately, the picture that the leaders, both religious and secular, pose is absolutely discouraging. That is why this new system has emerged in the world where love means sex, serving each other occurs only for monetary gain, and profit and justice is sought through unnecessary war, invasion in the name of peace, and senseless killing by terrorism.

Some may say, "Well, there is so much charity going on in the world. What about it?" My answer is have we really stopped to think or investigate and compare the percentage between the problems of the world and the relief that is meted out to overcome them? With all the charity that has been collected and still is being collected every day, poverty should have been eradicated by now. The irony is that, in spite of all the efforts, the poor remain poor and the rich are getting richer by leaps and bounds. Why?

Why is this all happening? Well, as mentioned earlier, the truth mentioned in the Bible is coming true word by word. God indeed has stepped back because of human arrogance and is allowing human beings to govern this world according to their design—apart from God's statutes—so that they will learn the difference when Jesus rules this world according to God's statutes and hopefully will change and achieve our own salvation.

So is Jesus true God and true man? I believe so because since five major religions (that I know of) vouch on his behalf, I find no room for disbelief. When I am in doubt, I repeatedly remind and question myself why would these religions who compete with each other (for supremacy so to say) have not deleted this truth from their holy books? If they do not believe in it and therefore do not preach this truth, then why are they still holding on to it?

The hands-on experience that I have gained and the knowledge I have gathered through extensive reading in the past twenty years has caused me to trust in the teaching of chapter 22 of the book of Revelation. It has encouraged me to settle down in peace and tranquility until I am called to depart from this world. I now live in full faith in God's assurance that I will rest peacefully in an appointed place. It encourages me to hope that Jesus will find me worthy to give entry into the New Heaven and New Earth and choose me to serve him in whatever capacity he feels fit, provided I follow his bidding. In all earnestly, I have been working toward this goal from the time my eyes where opened fifteen years ago.

"The Angel also showed me the river of the water of life, sparkling like crystal, and coming from the throne of God and of the Lamb and flowing down the middle of the city's street. On each side of the river was the tree of life, which bears fruit twelve times a year, once each month; and its leaves are for the healing of the nations. Nothing that is under God's curse will be found in the city. The throne of God and of the Lamb will be in the city, and his servants will worship him. They will see his face, and his name will be written on their forehead. There will be no more night, and they will not need lamps or sunlight, because the Lord will be their light and they will rule as kings for ever and ever. Then the Angel said to me, these words are true and can be trusted. And the Lord God, who gives his Spirit to the Prophets has sent his Angel to show his servant what must happen very soon" (Revelation 22:1-6).

The Lord said, "I am the Lord your God, worship no God but me. Do not make for yourselves images of anything in heaven and on earth and in the water and under the earth. Do not bow down to any idol or worship it, for I am the Lord your God and I tolerate no rivals. I bring punishment on those who hate me and on their descendents down to the third and fourth generations. But I show my love to thousands of generations of those who love me and obey my laws. Do not use my name for evil purposes, for I, the Lord your God will punish anyone who misuses my name" (Deuteronomy 5:6-11). Idols in the current sense not only mean real idols but also all worldly things.

And he said, "Do not keep the prophetic words of this book a secret, because the time is near [very near indeed] when all this will happen" (Revelation 22:10).

He said to them, "Go throughout the whole world and proclaim the Gospel to all mankind" (Mark 16:15).

This is what I have tried to do; I have tried to spread the truth to my readers because "'listen,' says Jesus, 'I am coming soon. Happy are those who obey the prophetic words of this book'" (Revelation 22:7).

Again in Revelation 22:12-13 Jesus says, "I am coming soon. I will bring my rewards with me, to give each one according to what he has done. I am the Alpha and the Omega, First and the Last, the Beginning and the End."

May God bless us all!

Author Biography

Oswald Sequeira (Ozzie) was born in 1943 in Mangalore City, situated on the west coast of Karnataka State in South India. He is an electrical engineer by profession. His career took him to East Africa and then to Abu Dhabi (Middle East). Presently, he is settled in Toronto, Canada, with his wife and two sons.

A miraculous healing of his left leg, incapacitated by an accident in 1994, at a retreat center in India caused a 360-degree turn in the life of this worldly man to God and faith.

Shortly after settling in Canada in 1996, he was diagnosed with advanced prostrate cancer along with four major blocks in an already-damaged heart due to a previously undiagnosed silent heart attack. Though it was a challenging case for the medical professionals, Ozzie's faith and prayers and the prayers of his loved ones and friends pulled him through. Ozzie considers this to be another miracle in his life.

As a token of gratitude, he volunteers for the Canadian Cancer Society and has pledged part of his earnings from this book for cancer research.

After his encounter with death, his passion for reading switched from fiction to history, science, and religious books. The result is *Alpha and Omega*—a must-read book. It covers *all of our histories*, from Adam to present day, in a concise form. The author backs up his conclusions with credible proof, encouraging the reader to pause and reflect. Subject matter is presented in a similar concise and easily understandable manner, thus enabling his readers to avoid the hassle of cross-referencing multiple books. This book is an excellent resource for those seeking to delve into the history of the Bible and presents readers with a unique opportunity to understand these truths in a simple, easy-to-understand reference.

Edwards Brothers,Inc!
Thorofare, NJ 08086
15 June, 2010
BA2010166